Powerful Thinking
on Purpose
For
Athletes

Harness The Power Of Your Mind
To Win Your Inner Game

By Wendy Merron

Cover design by Justin Turpin
Copyright © 2022 Wendy Merron
SportsRecoveryHypnosis.com

Dedicated to Justin Turpin and Grace Capuzzi
Two wonderful friends who are also amazing
Certified Hypnotists

Table of Contents

Introduction

Jake, a top-ranked golfer, was distressed about his game. Every time he practiced, he focused easily and his shots were consistent. But the moment he went to golf with his friends or in a tournament, his mind automatically went into negative territory and he couldn't stop overthinking.

He knew he suffered from some sort of mental block. He knew he should stop worrying about each shot. His busy brain was all over the place and seemed unable to maintain the mindset of confidence he knew he needed. His game was suffering. His mood felt erratic. He had no idea what to do. He just couldn't stop worrying that he would play poorly yet again.

He met with a Sports Psychologist, watched videos, listened to music, and even tried positive self-talk. Nothing seemed to make a difference.

His thoughts were uncharacteristically out of control. His sleep was erratic and he was afraid he lost his edge. He was tired of his self-defeating thoughts. His family and friends were sick of his complaints.

By the time he called me, he was so discouraged he wondered if this was time to end his career.

Through the process I explain in this book, Jake was able to regain control over his thoughts and improve his golf game. He learned to remain focused. His outlook improved. In addition to feeling less stressed, he began to sleep better, play more consistently, and woke up in the morning more optimistic. He was a new man; calmer, happier, and more positive.

Jake is one of many clients who experienced a significant improvement in his game and his life as a result of using Powerful Thinking on Purpose.

Have you ever met anyone who you consider to be a negative thinker? I'm sure you can think of a friend, relative, or colleague who seems to always think this way—continually moping about things going wrong, how difficult life is, or complaining about how others treat him. You probably don't enjoy spending time with this person. When you are with this person, you might think "If he could just think more positively, things might be different"?

Most likely, you aren't as negative as this person, but I bet you can recall times in your life when you were anxious and worried that things wouldn't work out the way you wanted. Regardless of what actually happened, you probably spent countless minutes, hours, or even days, in the throes of worry and anxiety that things won't get better.

If I told you changing your thoughts can help you improve would you believe me? I hope so because it's true. Not because I say it's true. It's true because hundreds of top athletes over the years have experienced major improvements in their sport when they learned to intentionally direct their thoughts.

As a Coach and Board Certified Hypnotist, one of my goals is to empower my clients with strategies to improve their game. Another goal is to help my clients overcome mental blocks. I do this by helping them discover the thoughts and what they imagine in their mind have a profound effect on their nervous system and their sport. I've helped amateur and professional athletes to create the mindset and strategies to achieve their goals.

I don't mean to sound like I'm an amazing person just because I've helped so many improve their lives. It's simply that the tools and techniques I teach clients are based on science and are incredibly effective and easy to use. Once you learn a few simple concepts.

Most athletes who seek me out are quite successful in more than one aspect of their life, whether personal or professional. The common thread is all of them are struggling in some aspect of their life and the known source of their struggle is their thinking process.

When athletes learn and use the powerful technique outlined in this book, they quickly notice a positive change in their feelings – they are aware they now react differently and their focus, and performance improves. Their old worries no longer affect their performance because they have learned what is necessary to change their thinking to achieve their goal.

Most mention at their second session they notice their performance is starting to improve. One client said it was as if a switch turned on and cleared her mind of the heavy gray clouds. She felt much more positive and open to possibilities that things would be OK.

Throughout this book, not only will you learn why it's important to change your thinking, you'll learn how to integrate a simple and powerful tool into your life to help you recover faster and greatly improve your performance.

By the way, none of this is difficult. It's just you haven't learned yet how to make the thought changes necessary to improve. Keep reading - you'll get there!

This book teaches you to transition from the way you currently think to intentionally transforming your thinking to improve your sport through Powerful Thinking on Purpose. When you can hold believable positive thoughts in your mind and focus on the outcomes you desire, you can achieve almost any goal without struggling. The trick is to purposefully change your thoughts by replacing them <u>properly</u> with powerful new thoughts.

My goal is to help you utilize these scientifically proven helpful techniques to improve your performance. And, of course, to feel happier. As you read, I expect you will have a few "AHA" moments, where the knowledge you already have becomes amazingly clear. You may also have a few affirming moments when you realize you are on the path of creating a powerful mindset which will improve your sport and your life.

This is what Powerful Thinking is all about. Learning how you can control your thoughts - and no longer allowing them to control you.

What is Positive Thinking?

It's difficult to explain what positive thinking means. Most of us describe positive thinking as the opposite of negative thinking:

"Positive thinking is when I don't think about negative thoughts."

"Positive thinking is using my mind to reach my goal without letting negative thoughts or insecurities get in my way."

The definition of the word "positive" according to the Merriam-Webster Dictionary is:

Positive: Contributing toward or characterized by an increase or progression

To me, positive thinking means to concentrate on something which is constructive and helpful. It means you are using your thoughts to move forward in the direction of your goals and desires. This is also called self-talk. Unfortunately, positive thinking only goes so far. Positive thinking and self-talk don't always work.

Self-talk can be the most motivational and powerful tool an athlete owns. Unfortunately, self-talk can cause an athlete to spiral down into poor performance."

There are two kinds of self-talk: Positive, and Negative

You already know what negative self-talk sounds and feels like. Anytime anger, doubt, fear, frustration, or anxiety enters your mind, you are in the company of negative self-talk.

Most athletes learn that positive self-talk is helpful. You've probably heard this from your family, friends, and coaches, from the moment you started training.

But there is a big problem with positive self-talk you may not know. I'm going to reveal how to overcome this problem so you can be the best you can be.

Powerful Thinking

Powerful Thinking is a new technique you will discover which helps you maintain a new positive focus on a specific, desired outcome. Powerful Thinking on Purpose is easy to learn and implement. Once you begin to use it and notice how your performance improves, it will be easy for you to remember to use it daily.

By the end of this book, you will be creating new, powerful positive thoughts to replace those old worries and anxiety about your performance and your future.

You've learned a lot from the experts in your field. How to visualize, how to do your sport, how to move correctly, how to strategize, and how to do what you need to win. Until now, no one has ever taught you how to overcome a fear or create the inner confidence you need to improve your performance and win.

That is what you are about to learn, step-by-step.

When you start to practice this new way of thinking, you may notice a feeling of lightness and optimism you haven't felt for a long time. Feeling positive is the first step to creating an effective powerful permanent mindset to improve your performance.

Does this mean when you think positively, you become unrealistic and overly optimistic? Will you be viewing the world through "rose-colored glasses"? Not necessarily. In order to be effective though, your positive thoughts need to be believable.

In my definition, thinking powerfully is a process focused on the desired end result. If I told you every thought which goes through my mind is positive, I'd be lying. If I told you once you learn these techniques, you will never have to think about your thoughts again, it would be untrue. But you can control and ultimately reduce those thoughts tremendously so if one pops up, it has no impact on your performance or your life.

The reality is you have thousands of thoughts each day and you are always going to experience negative thoughts. It's totally normal. The difference is now you will be more and more aware of your thoughts every time you train, practice, and play your sport. This new awareness is the first step to making the powerful thought changes needed to improve.

It goes without saying that if you don't change what you are doing now, you will be stuck where you are.

The processes which you'll be learning are approaches I have discovered or developed throughout the decades of helping my clients. These are also the same tools and techniques I teach each and every athlete in my practice. Some of the processes I describe you will use daily and others less frequently.

There are dozens of ways to change and create new thoughts and images to improve. This book is a compilation of the ways I have found to be the easiest and most effective. To become a Powerful Thinker is to intentionally control and direct your thoughts to improve your sport without struggling.

When you take your time to learn and use these techniques, you will notice some measurable benefits:

- Improved focus
- Ability to stay in the zone
- Improved concentration
- Ability to respond to opportunities more quickly
- Increased performance
- Increased self-confidence
- Decreased anxiety

Powerful Thinking on Purpose is the bridge from your current reality to believable improvement and outcomes. Will you wake up tomorrow and be the best, fastest, or strongest? Probably not. (You still have to practice of course!) But you can wake up tomorrow feeling better, more optimistic, knowing exactly what you need and how to practice inside your mind to improve your performance.

Chapter 1
Everything Starts With a Thought

A thought is what happens when your mind actively forms connected ideas. Merriam Webster defines thinking as "to form or have in the mind" and a thought as 1: the process of thinking, 2: serious consideration, 3: reasoning power, 4: the power to imagine.

Unfortunately, we can't see a thought, nor can we hold a thought in our hands. But, we can see the results of a thought. When you do something over and over, it becomes second nature or subconscious. It's similar to the repetition you use to create muscle memory. Every new thought creates something called a neural pathway in your mind. Neural pathways look a bit like tiny roots growing. Your mind is full of them. When you have the same thought over and over, your neural pathway becomes thicker. Using medical technology, we can actually view these neural pathways forming in the mind.

Thoughts don't have a physical structure, weight, or color. Some thoughts are like wisps of smoke, disappearing long before we are aware of them. Other thoughts feel so stuck in our minds it seems it would be easier to move a sleeping elephant than stop that thought. Many thoughts just repeat over and over in our minds. No one has been able to prove the existence of thoughts, but we know they exist.

Every day we repeat hundreds of thoughts. How many times have you noticed repeating one thought to yourself?

DID YOU KNOW?

If you have a thought every one to four seconds, you have between 14,400 - 57,600 thoughts per day.

An estimated 95% are repetitive negative thoughts.

Here are some repetitive negative thoughts about the future you may recognize:

I'm worried I'm already the best I'll ever be.

I can't do this.

I'm anxious I'll be off the team.

I'm afraid others are faster/stronger than me.

What if I fail?

I'm worried I won't have the career I've dreamed of.

No one will ever choose me.

What if I get hurt again?
What if I make a mistake again?

What if it's too hard?

Below are some repetitive positive thoughts about the future:

Hey! How come there are no positive thoughts up there?

There are none because most people don't have many positive thoughts about the future, (unless they are thinking fondly about a loved one, going on vacation, or anticipating something great). If they do, those thoughts rarely repeat throughout the day.

Take a moment and think about the future of the world. What was your first thought? Did you imagine a pleasant scene or one which made you worry?

Do you want to be just like the others who never get out of their negative thinking box? Of course, you don't. You want your life to be satisfying, fulfilling, and full of success and love. Other people live the lives they desire, why can't you?

The people who are fulfilled and enjoying their lives tremendously are doing something differently than you. Only a small percentage do this naturally. The rest of us have to choose to take control and direct our thoughts every day to feel great.

Athletes who learn to take control and direct their thoughts not only feel better, they tend to excel in their sport. They never get stuck in old negative mindsets which incessantly replay. More importantly, they enjoy their sport (and their lives) more.

Can Mental Practice Improve Performance?

Students from four Michigan High Schools participated in a study to determine the effect of mental practice compared with that of physical practice in the development of the 1-hand foul shot.

144 students were divided by their basketball experience: Varsity, Jr. Varsity, and Novice.

- 72 students from each group practiced 25 foul shots daily for 14 days
- 72 students MENTALLY IMAGINED practicing 25 foul shots daily (no physical practice) for 14 days

After 14 days of practicing 25 foul shots daily:

The Varsity group improved by	16%
The Jr. Varsity group improved by	24%

After 14 days of MENTALLY practicing only:

The Varsity group improved by	15%
The Jr. Varsity group improved by	23%

(The varsity and junior varsity groups scored higher than the novice group possibly because the novice group had minimal experience with basketball.)

Clark, L. V. (1960). Effect of mental practice on the development of a certain motor skill. <u>Research Quarterly of the American Association for Health, Physical Education, & Recreation,</u> 31, 560–569.

Highly successful athletes are those who know how to create, repeat and reinforce positive thoughts in their minds.

They know the value of taking control of their thoughts rather than letting their thoughts control them.

This is what Powerful Thinking on Purpose will teach you.

"Make sure your worst enemy doesn't live between your ears."
-Laird Hamilton, Big Wave Surfer, pioneer of tow-in surfing

Imagine your favorite basketball player is sitting on a bench in the locker room, right before an important game. He's hunched forward - his head in his hands. He worries his shot will be off - just like the last time. He's been in a slump and can't get out. In his mind, he shoots the ball. He imagines the ball bouncing off the rim. That uncomfortable scene replays over and over in his mind. The more he thinks about it, the worse he feels.

It's now time to play. He walks onto the court and tries to shake this unwanted scene out of his mind. What kind of game do you think he'll play? Most likely not his best.

Rewind that thought and imagine the same basketball player sitting on the bench prior to a game, this time his eyes are shut and he has a slight smile on his face. He actively and intentionally creates a short powerful film in his mind. In his mind he sees himself shooting the ball and his hands punch the air with excitement as the basketball cleanly swishes through the net. In the background, he hears the crowd cheering wildly and feels his teammates slap him on the shoulder. He makes his video bigger and brighter and watches it again.

His face breaks into a wide grin as he imagines his success.

Ready to get out and play, he struts onto the court smiling, shoulders back, feeling confident. Do you think he'll play a great game? Of course, he will!

We can learn two important facts from our basketball player:

1. Whatever he creates in his mind is bound to happen.
2. He feels better (and generally plays better) when he chooses to focus on what he wants.

Did you know some negative thoughts can seriously affect the physical body? The longer these negative thoughts and feelings stay stuck inside, the worse someone can feel. Years of guilt and regret can even manifest in physical ailments like stomach problems or chronic headaches.

Over time, constant repetitive worries and stress can weaken the immune system which makes it harder for the body to fight off viruses and bacteria.

Fear is a common feeling which often causes physical sensations. A particularly common one is the fear of public speaking.

Have you ever known someone who was extremely nervous and anxious about giving an upcoming presentation or speech?

Repetitive worry and anxiety about speaking can cause some people to feel so nervous and anxious their heart rate increases, their hands sweat, they lose sleep, or worse. They might even feel so bad they won't even show up for their own presentation.

Other common fears you may have experienced are the fear of getting hurt, making mistakes, playing badly, the fear of failure, and losing focus.

Take a moment and think about any fears or worries that have shown up for you recently.

You Can Be in Control of Your Thoughts

This may sound silly, but being aware of your thoughts is your first step.

Frankly, it's easy to go through your day running from here to there and keeping your life together, all the while not being aware of one thought. Maybe you even know some people who have bad habits which distract them from their thoughts and what's happening in their lives. Drinking, drugs, smoking, overeating, and watching videos are among the more popular. You might easily notice how you feel

—good, calm, anxious, frustrated, etc.—but not aware of your thoughts.

Once you are aware of your thoughts, it's easy to take the next powerful step: changing them. Keep in mind as you are becoming more aware, it's important to remember that you can be in total control of your thoughts. No one else can take control of them except you.

SUCCESS STORY

Tennis great Pete Sampras, who retired in August 2003 after a stunning career, used positive self-talk to remind himself that he could conquer an opponent even if he was behind and not playing well.

He often reminded himself that he has been on this court before, played the same opponent, and now needs to shift gears with some positive self-talk reminders that "everything is okay."

Anytime you take a deep breath and acknowledge something good and beneficial in your life, you are doing your mind and body a lovely favor. This is because you are taking a brief moment from your busy, stressful day to focus on a thought which feels good. Thoughts that feel good translate into a body that feels good. Your body is hardwired to work this way.

The Mind Body connection is real.

You Always Have a Choice

You can choose to think about the future in a negative way:

What if it takes too long to heal?

You can choose to think about the future in a positive way:

I'm glad I have good doctors.

You can choose to think about the past and experience negative feelings:

I am so annoyed I got hurt last week. What if I never recover as strong?

You can choose to think about the past and have a positive feeling:

I'm glad I'm getting stronger every day.

Did you notice the most repeated word in those sentences?

The word is *"choose."*

Of course, you can also choose to think about the present moment, which has tremendous benefits. This is called "mindful thinking." This way of thinking invites reflection in the moment and ultimately creates an implicit awareness of more than one perspective.

There are hundreds of books, websites, and many classes available to learn mindful thinking. For our purposes though, we will be focusing only on negative and positive thoughts.

Most people have no idea they can control their thoughts. For many, it's a revelation when they learn they can stop a negative thought and choose to replace it with a positive thought.

The truth is our thoughts are the only thing we have total control over.

No one can ever take this away from you. By the conclusion of this book, you will easily choose to change your thoughts every day and be surprised when you notice how your outlook improves.

Let's review the different kinds of thoughts about the future:

1.   Negative thoughts about the future.
2.   Positive thoughts about the future.

Here is the problem with negative thoughts about the future:

Every time one enters your mind,
it's guaranteed to make you feel bad.

Throughout this book, you will learn how to stop those annoying worries and anxieties that take over your thoughts.

You will learn the easiest way to change your negative thoughts into positive thoughts.

You will learn to take control over your thoughts - rather than those old worries and anxieties controlling you.

The beauty of Powerful Thinking on Purpose is it is simple and it always works. Whether you believe it works or not.

Just as you have bought this book to explore new ways to improve your life, you can easily choose to change and improve your thoughts. For example, if you are running a race tomorrow, you might have been saying to yourself:

I'm worried I won't do well

You'll be able to quickly change your thought to one which empowers you and causes a good feeling in the moment. For example, when you choose to think:

I like the idea I'll do great in tomorrow's race

you create the space to be the best you can be and your nervous system will send your body good feelings. You'll feel great while you think about your positive outcome and all the good feelings which result from finishing an amazing race.

Notice how good it feels when you choose an even bigger thought, such as

I like the idea I easily exceed my best time tomorrow.

The key to choosing and replacing negative thoughts with positive ones is your new thoughts MUST be believable.

What's impressive about Powerful Thinking on Purpose is the more you practice, the better you'll feel. The better you feel, the more you practice, and the easier it becomes. It's human nature to get better with practice.

With each new thought, you create new neural pathways in your mind. The more you practice Powerful Thinking on Purpose, the more you reinforce these neural pathways so your subconscious mind begins to think this way naturally, without prompting.

Chapter 2
The Secret Garden in Your Mind

Your Conscious Mind

There are two distinct parts of your mind: your subconscious mind and your conscious mind. Your conscious mind is the part of you that is responsible for logic and reason. If I asked you to tell me the weather is outside, or how to delete a file on your computer, you would come up with the answer by using your conscious mind.

Your conscious mind is also in charge of your daily analytical and critical thinking. It contains only what you are focusing in that moment. It's the part of you that asks questions, makes decisions, operates your computer, reads books, and handles day-to-day tasks. Judgment and choice both arise from your conscious mind. You use your conscious mind to make thousands of daily decisions.

An important fact is your conscious mind sends instructions to your subconscious mind.

Scientists have been studying the conscious and subconscious mind for decades. It's no surprise this is one area of science that continues to be challenging for researchers. Scientists generally agree the conscious mind, at any given moment holds only a small amount of information. According to Nelson Cowan[1], our conscious mind's working capacity to hold information is limited to a mere three or four items.

Your Subconscious Mind

On the other side of your mind, your subconscious contains a huge amount of stuff. This part of your mind holds all your memories, experiences, emotions, and in addition, your vast imagination. Everything you have heard, seen, felt, tasted, touched, smelled, and experienced in your life is stored here and can be accessed faster than you can blink.

Four important facts about your subconscious mind are

1. Your subconscious mind holds all of your feelings and emotions.
2. Your imagination resides in your subconscious mind.
3. Everything you have experienced (your memory) is held in your subconscious mind.
4. Your subconscious mind takes instructions from your conscious mind.

[1] The Magical Number 4 in Short-Term Memory: A Reconsideration of Mental Storage Capacity, Behavioral and Brain Sciences, Vol. 24, No. 1, pages 87-114, Feb. 2001

Here is where things get tricky: Your subconscious mind is the part designed to protect you and is always in control. It will never sabotage you, but I bet sometimes it feels as if that's happening.

When you hold negative thoughts and worries in your conscious mind, your subconscious mind believes this is how you want to feel. It will do everything in its power to make sure you get what it thinks you want. That may not seem right, but when you get to the end of this book, it will make total sense.

Your subconscious thinks you want to feel anxious and worried, so it will make sure this happens. Yikes. That's NOT what you want. The truth is your life reflects your thoughts. Your outer experience mirrors what your inner thoughts create.

If you ever wonder what your thoughts have been, take an honest look at your life right now. Your life reflects your thoughts and beliefs as they are held in your mind.

"Our minds become magnetized with the dominating thoughts we hold in our minds and these magnets attract to us the forces, the people, the circumstances of life which harmonize with the nature of our dominating thoughts."
-Napoleon Hill

All of your beliefs, experiences, and expectations are stored in your subconscious mind. Your subconscious mind holds a vast amount of information and it generates your emotional responses based on its experiences. This is the part of your mind where you have the ability to make profound and lasting changes.

Ever wonder why some people scream when they see a spider or a mouse? Their subconscious mind is reacting to an old thought, belief, or fear. In reality, if that person would use their conscious mind to think analytically, he might realize that a mouse, much weaker and smaller than a human, really can't do any harm. When you respond to situations like that, you always react with your subconscious mind, not your logical, analytical conscious mind.

If you overreact in a situation, it's because your subconscious mind is reacting to an old thought or belief. This is called "being triggered".

I like to explain to clients their subconscious mind has no opinions and is similar to a garden. The ground in your garden has no opinions either.

Imagine you're preparing to plant some blue Forget-Mc-Not flower seeds in the corner of your garden. You thoughtfully choose the perfect location, use your shovel to prepare the soil, and gently drop the seeds into the ground. You carefully cover the seeds with dirt and take the time to regularly water the new seeds regularly.

While you were planting, not once did the ground in your garden ever say to you:

"Hey, are you SURE you want those blue flowers over there? It's really not a good place for them. They will grow much better over there near the large tree. And I've got to let you know these are going to become little blue flowers and your favorite color is pink. Are you sure this is what you really want?"

Of course, your garden will never utter a word. Your garden will simply accept the seeds, nurture them and allow the seeds to take root and grow. The ground in your garden voices no opinions the same way your subconscious mind has no opinions.

After planting your seeds, you water your Forget-Me-Nots frequently and the roots begin to grow. These pretty little blue flowers begin to sprout and grow larger. You know whatever you plant and water in your garden, whether flowers, vegetables, bushes, or trees, all will grow. Some plants grow quickly. Others take longer.

So what does this have to do with your subconscious mind? When you were young, your mind was very much like this garden. Thoughts, ideas, and beliefs took seed in your garden every day.

Like a garden accepting a plant, your mind accepted many beliefs without question. Of course, your mind never responded by replying:

Are you SURE you want to believe this?

In my practice, I frequently help people who want to overcome their fear of reinjury or improve their performance. After helping thousands of clients, I've noticed most people's fears took root in their subconscious minds at an early age.

When you are young and internalize a new belief, no matter how outlandish or unfounded, or where it came from, your subconscious mind often unquestionably accepts this new belief as truth.

And unless something happens to change it, this belief can remain in your subconscious mind for years or even decades.

DID YOU KNOW?

The same way plants and flowers attract birds, bees, butterflies, and insects, the thoughts in your mind attract things.
Negative thoughts tend to attract negative outcomes, causing unhappiness and misery.
Positive thoughts tend to attract opportunities, possibilities, improvement, and happiness.

Your subconscious mind is an extremely important part of you because it stores your imagination, thoughts, and feelings. You wouldn't be who you are if you didn't have a subconscious mind. It is also a fierce protector. If you want to do something which is in conflict with your subconscious beliefs, your subconscious will do everything in its power to make sure it won't happen.

In Chapter 13, Your Personal Protector, you'll learn how your subconscious mind sometimes stops you from doing what you want.

Chapter 3
Don't Think of a Pink Elephant

Imagine you are the captain of a massive ship. You are in charge of determining where the ship will go, how fast to go, and the destination. You are a great captain, but, you can't sail this ship on your own.

You are the "Conscious Mind" Captain. You are brilliant. You ask questions, you are objective, you think. You are aware.

The ship also holds an amazing crew of thousands who will do everything you ask - without question.

Your crew is your subconscious mind.

Your crew takes things literally, which means you MUST be very specific when you communicate with it. Your subconscious is always in the present, responding to instructions from the thoughts you hold in your mind.

Your crew's job is the carry out the instructions they receive from you, the captain. They do this beautifully. Every day. Without fail. Without questioning you.

But…you have to ask them in the right way. If you don't pay attention to this one extremely important thing, you'll never get what you want.

Your crew has been trained to do things in a certain way. They will keep on doing what they have been trained to do until they learn to do something better.

Your job now is to retrain your crew. And just like training for your sport requires practice, you'll be using practice to train your crew.

This is what Powerful Thinking is all about and I'm going to teach you how to do this.

Here's something important for you to know:

The Pink Elephant

Imagine I am saying the following three sentences to you. Read all three of them first and then do them as an exercise:

1. Close your eyes.
2. Take a deep breath.
3. DON'T think of a pink elephant in your mind.

What just happened? Most likely, 75 percent of you briefly saw a pink elephant in your mind. The other 25 percent imagined a pink elephant for a brief moment and then quickly tried to erase it or turn their mind blank.

Either way, the image of a pink elephant appeared —even for a split second.

This occurred because your subconscious mind MUST imagine the pink elephant before you can delete it.

Essentially, your subconscious ignored the word "DON'T" and interpreted the last sentence as

Imagine a pink elephant in your mind.

This wasn't exactly what you intended. You wanted to make sure you DID NOT imagine a pink elephant!

If you are golfing and want to get the ball in the hole and you worry, "I don't want to miss a shot put again," the subconscious eliminates the word "don't" and interprets the thought like this:

I want to miss a shot put again.

If you think to yourself

Don't make a mistake.

Your inner mind interprets that as

Make a mistake.

This is what your subconscious mind hears and processes. That's NOT what you wanted! Yikes.

Of course not. No wonder things don't always work out the way you want!

How you talk to yourself is essential to your personal success or failure. The words you choose are extremely important in achieving your goal.

Read the two sentences below. Which one do you think will work best to help you reach your goal?

A) I don't want to miss the shot put again.

B) I choose to stay calm and relaxed and get the shot I want.

If you answered B) you now understand the power of self-talk and the power of your words.

What do you think will happen when you instruct your crew

"Don't stop the ship at 10:00 AM." ?

(Remember, your crew takes you literally, and doesn't recognize the word "don't".)

Your crew will stop your ship at 10:00 AM.

Definitely NOT what you wanted.

It is always more effective to focus on the outcome you desire because your subconscious mind often ignores negative words. Anytime your subconscious hears a negative word such as "don't" or "won't," these words are as good as ignored.

To put it simply

> When you think about what you want,
> you get what you want.

> When you think about what you don't want,
> you get what you don't want.

You've been doing this your whole life

When you reflect on your personal success, how did you obtain the mindset to achieve your goal? You probably didn't do anything other than think about what you wanted.. You simply took the next step.

Once you had your initial thought, were you inundated with worry or fear you might fail? Or were you confident you could get where you wanted to go? Maybe your thoughts went back and forth, from excitement to worry.

It's normal for everyone to have worries and concerns.
What you do with those worries and concerns has everything to do with your success—in life and in your sport.

I bet you know some people who are the worst negative thinkers around. Constantly grumbling about how things don't work out for them. Focusing on their overwhelmed lives, living with their "glass half full." Have you ever wondered, "If he/she could be more positive, things might be so much easier…"?

When you set a goal for yourself, for example, to set a personal best, the first thing that enters your mind is how good it will feel or what it will look like.

If you start to hold on to thoughts of doubt and worry you'll never achieve that, then I guarantee you will never achieve that.

The reason why negative thoughts create negative reactions has to do with the science of how your subconscious mind works.

Your subconscious mind takes instructions from your conscious mind. In fact, it receives every thought as a direction from you. It receives those instructions via thoughts, words, and feelings. That's the language it understands.

Just like your computer takes instructions from the text you input. Your computer doesn't question you. It just gives you *what it thinks you want.* To get what you want from your computer, you have to be clear with your request.

Your inner subconscious mind works the same way.

Here's what happens - in slow motion...

First, you have a worrying thought

"I'm worried I'm not good enough and won't do well."

Next, your subconscious mind, which is connected to your autonomic nervous system, receives that thought.

Your inner mind interprets that as a request that you want the worry and doubtful feelings. It has no opinion or judgment. It will NEVER respond with "Are you sure that is what you want?"

Your subconscious interprets this as instruction, from the conscious mind:

He wants to worry.

He thinks he's not good enough.
He thinks he won't do well.

He must want to worry.
He must want to think he's not good enough.
He must want to feel that he won't do well.

OK. Then, I (the subconscious mind) will inform his nervous system to send him those feelings.

And then... your nervous system sends you feelings so you continue to worry you are not good enough and won't do well.

WHAT???? THAT IS NUTS!!!

That is NOT what you want!

What you really, truly want is to feel optimistic that you can do what you are setting out to do!

But, you didn't have THAT thought, because that old worry automatically popped into your head and took root :-(

To retrain your thoughts, anytime you notice that worry, fear, anxiety, swipe it out of your mind and quickly replace it with your "I like the idea... statement.

You might be doing this 10, 50, or even 100 times a day in the beginning. (It's all in your mind, so no physical effort required.)

Each time will feel better than the last and after a week or so you'll notice how good you feel.

NOW YOU KNOW

When you say a sentence to yourself that includes the word "don't," your subconscious mind often cannot process or recognize it. It's as if the word is deleted from the sentence.

Chapter 4
5 Powerful Words

In my teens and twenties, I was the most miserable and negative person you could imagine. My thoughts bounced between worry, pessimism, and hopelessness. It was exhausting.

On any given day I had perhaps two positive thoughts. OK, that may be a bit of an exaggeration, but 90% of my thoughts were pessimistic. I worried about my career, my finances, my love life, and even the weather worried me. You name it, I could find something to worry about. Some weeks, the only positive thought I could muster was "Well, at least I have gas in my car."

Over time, I learned and developed the techniques detailed in this book. Because I now easily control and direct my thoughts, I would estimate now over 90 percent of my thoughts are positive and optimistic.

Let me be honest here. We never entirely get rid of worry and fear. It's not possible. What's possible is you can take control, move, shift and change these negative thoughts so you can be and feel better and they don't hang around as long as they used to.

When I was younger, I knew most people were much happier than me. It wasn't hard to tell the people who thought positive were more content and appeared to have fulfilling lives. Or maybe the people who were content and had fulfilling lives seemed happier. No matter what the cause, I wanted to feel better and be happier.

It was hard. I was unable to believe I could be happy in my life. I believed life wasn't fair. (Cue parent's voice here: "Life isn't fair. Get used to it.")

Life was difficult when I was young and I believed things would always continue to be difficult. This was my reality. Not a great place to hang out.

Deep inside, I knew instinctively if I could think in a different way, things might change. I could make myself feel better. So I tried to think differently.

I tried to pretend I was happy.

I tried to smile a lot.

I tried to feel good.

The more I tried different ways of feeling good and being positive, the more frustrated I became. I could only notice how deeply unhappy I was.

One day, in an effort to feel better, I tried the old "fake it till you make it" process. In my mind I thought

I am happy.

Immediately my inner mind retorted:

No, you're not. That's a load of crap.

Then I said to myself:

I want to be happy.

My inner voice responded with a snarl:

Well then, keep on wanting. Maybe when pigs fly you'll be happy.

In a huff of frustration, I thought:

I LIKE the idea that I can be happy.

And I waited.

And waited some more.
I heard nothing from my inner mind, only silence. It finally had nothing to refute. It was definitely a weird moment. I knew something was different.

Maybe I accepted that statement as truth?

I decided to repeat the sentence I LIKE the idea that I can be happy, over and over. For days, I said my sentence. In the beginning, it felt odd to think something I knew wasn't true. But I knew I wanted it - badly.

In a short time, I noticed a strange shift. The thought:

I like the idea that I can be happy.

had somehow taken root in my mind. I noticed tiny pockets of time when I truly DID feel happy. Nothing huge or earth-shattering. I wasn't 100 percent top-of-the-world ecstatic, but I was aware I occasionally felt better.

Somehow, the way I worded this statement was so different my subconscious mind accepted it much more easily. I realized I had stumbled upon something quite outstanding. The words:

I like the idea that...

caused my statement to feel true for me. Because I knew that I DID like that idea!

It struck me that if I really wanted to feel happy, adding these 5 Powerful Words to my statement created a monumental change. That phrase was true and I knew it was true. I believed it.

Rewording it caused it to become a thought which didn't meet with resistance. I was amazed this new, believable thought was so easily accepted into my subconscious mind without any resistance. It was a strange moment.

Trying It Out With a Client

When I am with my clients, I view our relationship as a partnership. I do my part 150%, and it's necessary for my client to do his or her part by reinforcing new thoughts and feelings. Twice a day each client spends about five minutes using his subconscious mind to install new powerful positive thoughts so he can achieve his goals.

Each client learns and experiences a personal step-by-step routine to powerfully rewire their mind. Clients do this by repeating their powerful personal statement and combining it with a specific, appropriate future visualization. (You'll learn this technique in Chapter 15).

A professional golfer came into my office stressed and frustrated. He had been in a slump for over two months. He was anxious and his game suffered. He was unable to stop the relentless overthinking which he knew affected his ability to play well.

After explaining how his conscious and subconscious minds communicated, I asked him to make up a personal goal. He replied

"I always do well in tournaments,"

I asked him to repeat this in his mind, and report to me on a scale of 0 to 100 percent how believable that statement seemed for him.

He said

"About 75 percent. But I really DO want this to be the truth. I do want to play well in tournaments."

OK, I thought. We're close, but not quite there. So instead of my golfer repeating:

"I always do well in tournaments."

I had him add the words "I like the idea that…"

"I like the idea that I always do well in tournaments."

He repeated it. Then he said it aloud. He repeated it. I asked him to tell me how believable it felt. He grinned.

"Of course it's believable! Because it's 100 percent believable to like that idea!"

Using the phrase "I like the idea that" immediately made a tremendous difference and his reaction was delightful. He was able to believe his Powerful Personal Statement even though he wasn't there yet.

His mental practice for the week was to combine his statement with an imagined specific future event. He practiced pretending to imagine how he would feel after he won a tournament. He diligently practiced for about five minutes twice a day.

The next time he walked into my office he was smiling. He reported he had a great week and played better than at any time in the past four months!

He also mentioned a concern.

"After a few days, I began to drop off the 'I like the idea that.' Is this okay?"

His question to me was proof his subconscious mind accepted his new, Powerful Personal Statement and after he internalized it, he naturally shortened it.

He no longer had to "like the idea" because his subconscious had adopted his new thought. At his core, he truly knew he could play better.

Because thoughts are the client's key to success, after the first session it's typical for clients to become more aware of their thinking patterns. They become more aware when they are stuck in a pattern of worry or anxiety. They notice more of those "what if" thoughts that tend to pop up every day. They also notice the difference in their feelings when they take control of their thoughts.

Many, unfortunately, hold a powerful lingering subconscious concern. A part of them may have a worry or fear they might not succeed, but of course, since this is subconscious, they are unaware. They simply know they don't feel good or optimistic.

My goal is to help my clients create new thoughts and beliefs so they can achieve their goals without struggling. Any resistance to a new thought will ultimately cause people to give up. My goal is to help them learn to bypass any subconscious resistance to their new statement.

I want to make sure what clients are repeating to themselves is believable. When a thought is 100 percent believable, then change and improvement can occur without resistance.

If it's not believable, it is the same as lying to ourselves. It's impossible to repeat a lie about ourselves. Lying to ourselves feels uncomfortable and we eventually stop saying that sentence.

As a result of my experience with my golfer, I realized I was onto something. I knew I had discovered a new way of phrasing powerful personal statements.

I discovered an efficient and simple way of permitting the subconscious mind to begin to accept a new thought without resistance.

I began sharing this with more and more athletes and I noticed they were feeling better, playing better, and experiencing benefits much more rapidly than before.

Adding the 5 Powerful Words to their personal statement made it easier to stay on track with their goals. They were achieving their goals with less stress.

And all it took was the addition of 5 Powerful Words:

I like the idea that…

I was delighted.

It's human nature to want to be successful and we like to seek help from those who have already achieved success. The first caveman helped his fellow man find shelter and food. These cavemen shared their knowledge about the land and, over time, taught others the benefits of fire for warmth and cooking.

As the number of people grew, people found more ways to help others. Early healers provided relief to their fellow man, from physical pain, hunger, and more. Physical healing was the primary aid but over time early people began to help each other with emotional healing too.

Throughout history, we've learned myriad techniques for physical and emotional healing. Positive self-talk and repeating affirmations are powerful techniques that have existed for thousands of years.

As long ago as 2000 years, the Egyptians used affirmations, self-talk, and healing suggestions in their sleep temples for the purpose of healing the mind and body.

While sleep temples are no longer around, they have been replaced by modern medicine and psychology. Today, because it's so easy, many people's first choice is to take a pill to feel emotionally better.

As each generation discovers and learns the power of thought, they pass this powerful information to the next generation. Through word of mouth, books, podcasts, movies, the internet, and more, many people now know that what we think has a direct effect on what we feel.

Day By Day In Every Way

If you were alive at the turn of the 20th century, you might have heard of a powerful self-help technique that was popularized by Émile Coué, a charismatic pharmacist and psychologist from
.

A commonly held belief at that time was that a strong, persistent willpower constituted the best path to success. Coué maintained that curing some of our troubles required a change in our subconscious thought. Only after we change our subconscious thoughts, can we place ourselves on the path to personal success.

While Coué was working as a pharmacist, he noticed that he could improve the efficiency of a medication by praising its effectiveness to his patients. He became aware that the patients for whom he praised the medication had a noticeable improvement when compared to the patients who simply received their medication without a suggestion.

While Coué believed in medication, he observed that his patients could heal themselves more efficiently by replacing a *"thought of illness"* with *"a thought of cure."* At the time, it was a new and unusual concept.

Coué believed that the repetition of words and images, once accepted by the subconscious mind, had the ability to heal both emotionally and physically.

He believed that what you think tended to become true for you. He realized that if one of his clients had been ill and still believed he was ill, then he would remain ill. Of course, he may not have been the first to realize this, but he was certainly one of the first to popularize the benefits of positive thinking and positive self-talk.

Coué wrote in his book, My Method and Self Mastery Through Conscious Autosuggestion, 1922,

Autosuggestion is as old as the hills; only we had forgotten to practice it and so we needed to learn it all over again. The power of thought, of idea, is ... immeasurable.

The world is dominated by thought. The human being individually is also entirely governed by his own thoughts, good or bad. The powerful action of the mind over the body which explains the effects of suggestion, was well known to the great thinkers of the Middle Ages, whose vigorous intelligence embraced the sum of human knowledge.

For a brief but spectacular period during the early '20s, this French apothecary's marvelously simple system of mental healing and his word-a-day theory of human personality captured the imagination of countless millions both in the U.S. and abroad. Overnight, Cou'és formula for recovery, "Day by day, in every way, I am getting better and better," became the stock phrase of the country.

Scholars have described Coué as the father of the American Positive Thinking movement.

By the time Coué arrived in the United States in 1923, he was so popular that a song was written about him by the famous Broadway duo of William Jerome and Jean Schwartz. Jerome H. Remick & Co. N.Y., published "Every Day in Every Way I'm Getting Better and Better, The Healthy Song". The song found its way to saloons and parlors across the country.

Here's the chorus for this popular song:

Day by day…in every way…
I'm getting better and better every day!

On cloudy days this mental exercise
will brighten up your eyes and bring you sunny skies…

Day by day…in every way…
it's surely easy, and not so hard to say…

Learn this simple-ist of rhymes and repeat it twenty times…

Day by Day, I'm getting better every day!

I bought a copy of the music score many years ago and recorded a friend singing it. We put the video on YouTube in 2011. It's the only one of its kind, and worth the three minute listen!

You can hear this rousing rendition on YouTube at https://youtu.be/UfqAM_a2Md0

DID YOU KNOW?

The famous singer and songwriter Johnny Cash remarked about the phrase "Every day in every way I'm getting better and better,"

"I didn't especially believe that about myself, but I said it every day and I made myself believe it and it worked. I never gave up my dream to sing on the radio. And that dream came true in 1955."

Chapter 5
What's Your Goal?

In order to achieve success, it's logical the first thing you must have in mind is a specific goal.

Every goal begins with a thought. To achieve success, your goal must be in total alignment with your beliefs and desires. It's not enough to have a goal of something you want to do, be, or have. First and foremost, your goal must be reasonable and believable to you. This is crucial to your success.

If your dream is to be the center of a National Basketball Association (NBA) team and you are only 5 feet tall, then your goal isn't very reasonable or believable, is it?

On the other hand, if your goal is to win a triathlon, and you are fit and love competing in swimming, biking, and running, then of course it's reasonable and believable.

SUCCESS STORY

German Madrazo was 43 when he competed in Cross Country Skiing during the Pyeongchang Winter Olympics. What is amazing is he took up skiing when he was 42 years old!

To be able to achieve his goal, he had to feel his goal was reasonable and believable.

If he had thought "I'm too old to compete, I'll never be able to finish," how far do you think he would have gone? Most likely, his negative thoughts would have stopped him from putting on his ski boots. German Madrazo kept the outcome he wanted in his thoughts and went on to ultimately qualify and compete in the Winter 2018 Olympic Games.

NOW YOU KNOW

When you are in control of your thoughts, you are in control of your life.

It's important to be aware of your negative thoughts because they have the power to get in the way of achieving your goals and desires. When you use the worksheets at the back of this book, you'll be on your way to bypassing those pesky, relentless negative thoughts so you can achieve your goals.

Set Your Personal Goal

Think about some of the personal goals you have set for yourself. Perhaps one of your goals is to overcome your fear of reinjury. You might have other long-term goals, such as improving your performance, making a team, learning a new skill, going on vacation, buying a house, making more money, finding your soul mate, writing a book, or even changing your career.

Short-term goals might be exercising for twenty minutes daily, or getting back into your sport or in the game.

Take a moment and think about what would make you feel happy and fulfilled. What going on in your life that you don't want? What do you want more of? This can help you solidify your various goals.

Start with Small Steps

Sometimes personal goals are so big they may feel unattainable.

For example, if you are seriously injured and expect you will be fully recovered and playing at full capacity in a week, you know that isn't possible.

A more realistic goal is to focus on increasing your strength a bit more every day.

Most people tend to do much better when they take small steps towards their goals.
(This reminds me of a joke my brother told me when he was seven: "How do you eat an elephant? [Answer:} One bite at a time!")

With each small step, you can easily achieve some success. And when you have achieved a little success, it's easier to reach the next step and the next step. Success enables more success. As you work through the sheets in the Appendix, you'll see how easy it is for you to take the next small step in your life to achieve your goal - whether it is related to your sport or your personal life.

Achieving success, even with something small, is terrific. Each success adds to the one before, and the more successes you experience, the more your confidence increases. When you are confident, you automatically increase your potential for success.

Set Your Personal Goal

Write 3 personal goals below (long or short term)

GOAL 1_____

GOAL 2_____

GOAL 3_____

What's important is to never lose sight of YOUR ultimate goal to:

- **Improve your performance**

- **Overcome your fears**

- **Get 100% back into your sport without fear of reinjury**

Healing from an injury takes time. Bouncing back from poor performance or a disappointing game or season takes time. You need time to strengthen your body. *You also need time to focus and strengthen your mind.*

If you fail to address both your body and mind, you'll never perform at your absolute best.

Taking small steps and intentionally focusing on the outcome you want, (rather than the worries and fears), will ultimately lead you to the success you desire.

SUCCESS STORY

Christina Clemons was 5th in the world in her sport, the 100 meter hurdle. She ruptured her Achilles in 2013. Unfortunately she failed to make the Olympic trials final in 2016. Fearing her past experience and her old injury would get in the way again, she contacted me (I'm a Board Certified Hypnotist) at The Center of Success in Wayne, PA, to help her achieve her goal of getting on the three-person Olympic team in 2021.

Through her sessions she learned how to properly visualize and create the mental imagery to increase her speed. She practiced her pre-race routine and her new mindset strategies daily. She was thrilled when during the trials she achieved her best time ever and gained her spot on the Olympic team!

If you are recovering from an injury you can

A)   Imagine checking in with your physician or physical therapist and imagining his or her surprise at how well you are doing or

B)   You could imagine you never fully recover.

If you are training hard to try out for a spot on the team you can

A)   Imagine how great you'll feel when you make it or

B)   You could worry you have no future career in your sport.

<u>You</u> know exactly what you want, so it's time to take the first step.

Putting your goal on paper is the first step to achieving it. (Putting it on paper makes it real.)

Write three personal goals (short-term or long-term) below:

My goal is_____.

My goal is_____.

My goal is_____.

Chapter 6
Based on Science

Can you imagine holding half of a lemon right now? Take a moment and pretend you are looking at the shiny yellow flesh. Pretend you can feel the bumpy feeling of the skin of that lemon. Now, imagine you are slowly bringing it closer and closer and closer to your mouth... now it touches your lips...QUICKLY - sink your teeth into that lemon... think of that tart, sour taste...mouth-watering... lemony taste...

If you were to imagine the lemon scene for a few more minutes, the thought of that lemon would lead to the activation of the same brain areas as if you were actually biting into that sour fruit. You would automatically start to feel your mouth water.

If I told you using visualization (or pretending to use your imagination) without exercise could actually make a physical change in your muscles, you probably wouldn't believe me. Stay with me, because what you will learn is going to surprise you and could be the biggest game changer in your life and your sport.

While witnessing your potential physical success in your mind's eye can help enhance focus and encourage confidence, visualizing regularly has remarkable benefits which reach beyond the purely mental.

Visualizing is simply repeatedly imagining what you want to achieve. It is one of the most powerful tools top athletes (and happy people) use on a regular basis.

You already know the power of visualizing.

But did you know you can actually prevent muscle weakness, tone your muscles, delay atrophy, and even make your muscles stronger *just by using mental imagery exercises?*

Here's what happened in a 2014 study conducted by researchers at the Ohio University Heritage College of Osteopathic Medicine.

Researchers started with two sets of healthy individuals.

One half of the group had one wrist wrapped in a cast to prevent them from moving their wrist. They were given instructions to sit still for 11 minutes, five days a week, for four weeks, and 'perform mental imagery of strong muscle contractions, that is, to simply imagine exercising.

The other half of the group was given no instructions. They were to do nothing.

At the end of the four weeks, the researchers noted that the participants who engaged in the mental exercise measured *twice the muscle strength* as those who did not.

Fascinating, yes? Keep reading, because there's more than one research study that proves how powerful mental exercise can be.

Using Imagination to Increase Muscle Strength

A study from the Cleveland Clinic Foundation in Ohio also revealed similar results.

Researchers divided 30 healthy young adults into 3 groups. For 15 minutes a day, five days a week for 12 weeks:

Group #1 imagined exercising their little finger muscle.
Group #2 imagined exercising their biceps muscle and
Group #3 acted as a control group and did no imaginary exercise.

The researchers measured muscle strength before, during, and after the training sessions.

Those in the first two groups were asked to think, feel and imagine as strongly as they could about moving their muscles. Each participant was asked to make the imaginary movement as real as possible. The results:

Group #1 (The finger exercisers) increased their strength by 53%

Group #2 (The bicep exercisers) increased their strength by 13.4%

The measurements of the participant's brain activity during each visualization session suggest these strength gains were due to improvements in the brain's ability to signal muscle activity. It does sound unbelievable, but it's true.

Can Bone Fractures Heal More Quickly Using Thought?

12 people with broken ankles were recruited for this study. None of the patients needed surgery and all were receiving treatment at Massachusetts General Hospital in Boston.

6 patients received hypnosis once a week for 12 weeks.
6 patients received no treatment.

Radiologists and physicians who treated the group did not know which patients underwent hypnosis.

RESULTS: Those who were hypnotized healed faster than those who were not. Six weeks after the fracture, those in the hypnosis group showed the equivalent of *eight and a half weeks of healing.*

Amazing, isn't it?

Ginandes, Carol S; Rosenthal, Daniel I. Using hypnosis to accelerate the healing of bone fractures: A randomized controlled pilot study. Alternative Therapies in Health and Medicine; Vol. 5, Iss. 2, (Mar 1999): 67-75.
Reported in The Harvard Gazette, May 8, 2003

Does this mean you no longer have to exercise and practice? Of course not.

However, using your mind in addition to physical practice can have measurable effects.

Chapter 7
Custom Made to Fit Every Time

Perhaps you are frustrated with where you are right now. Perhaps you are in rehab and recovering from an injury and worried about your future. May you want to improve your strength, speed, or performance? You might even feel you aren't improving fast enough. You don't know how to get out of this space.

What do you do? You go out and buy a book that promises your life will change. You read the book and are thrilled the author has experienced amazing and wonderful changes by using powerful sentences called affirmations. You begin to feel excited because you have a new path and the potential to change, just as the author has. After reading and studying the book in detail, you go for it.

You know you are as capable as the next athlete. You know others have achieved success and they are no better or worse than you. You deserve to live your dream life.

You read the book and decide to conscientiously follow the author's suggestions to practice daily. You know how important self-talk is. You don't skip a day. Every morning you wake up and read or recite the affirmations. You repeat them in the shower and while you exercise. Every night before you go to bed, you practice self-talk and repeat the affirmations again.

After a few weeks of dutifully repeating affirmations night and day, you know NOTHING has changed.

You feel no different than when you started.

You haven't improved your time, your distance, or your score.

You notice you feel the same way you did when you first purchased the book. You are your same old self. The same old repetitive worries take up space in your thoughts. Not much has changed.

You worry you'll never get to where you want. You worry you aren't good enough. Those same old worries and negative thoughts control you. The promised miracle hasn't occurred.

You feel discouraged and disheartened. Why does self-talk seem to work for other people and not for you? Did you do something wrong? You begin to feel you'll never get what you want in life. You sadly realize spending so much time on self-talk hasn't produced the miraculous changes you expected.

The promise that being positive will make a huge change in your life just hasn't materialized.

You decide to throw out anything to do with affirmations and look for another way to improve your thinking process.

Wait! Don't give up!

You didn't do anything wrong. There is a reason your thoughts about your future didn't change. There is a simple explanation for what went wrong.

As you begin to recognize and learn the secrets of Powerful Thinking on Purpose, you will find it really is easy to improve your thoughts to ultimately improve your performance or play without worrying about reinjury.

Nice to know, isn't it?

But I Don't Believe It

The reason self-talk and affirmations fail is most people hold a belief in their subconscious mind which prevents that affirmation from being accepted.

When you say an affirmation to yourself, such as:

I will come back stronger than ever

and your first thought is:

I like this idea, but… :-(

or

Part of me doesn't think it's possible…

I guarantee you'll never achieve your goal.

In the following chapters, you'll learn the elements needed to create your own highly effective Powerful Personal Statements. At the same time, you'll be guided to learn step-by-step what you need to achieve your goals.

The Importance of Customization

FACT: It's your life and only your personal statements will work for you.

Sentences and phrases written by someone else won't work for you. Your coach's affirmations won't work for you; a teammate's won't work for you. The simple secret is only yours will work for you.

SUCCESS STORY

MARY LOU RETTON, GYMNASTIC OLYMPIC GOLD METAL WINNER

Six weeks before the Olympics Retton suffered a knee injury which required surgery.

During her time in physical therapy, and right up to the Olympics, she often would lay in her bed mentally imagining herself perform. She imagined performing her best routines over and over on each piece of equipment. She saw and felt herself in perfect form, executing every move cleanly. Retton even went as far as to imagine receiving the gold medal, and hearing the "Star-Spangled Banner" booming in the background. Did her mental rehearsals make a difference? Absolutely. She won the gold metal in 1984 in gymnastics, only six weeks after a major knee surgery.

Customizing your Personal Statement is an important part of positive change. You get a much greater reward when you learn how to create your own rather than using someone else's. Your Powerful Personal Statement will work much more rapidly because yours is customized to bypass any personal (and subconscious) resistance you might be holding.

What I mean by resistance is any personal thoughts or beliefs which may get in the way of achieving your desires. I'll be talking about this later in more detail in Chapter 11, Getting Stuck by Limiting Beliefs.

Remember: YOUR Powerful Personal Statement will always fit YOU quite well. It won't, however, fit your friends or your neighbors as well as it will fit you.

Powerful Personal Statements are like custom mouth guards, golf clubs, or sneakers. When you use someone else's, it feels uncomfortable. It's human nature to avoid what's uncomfortable so eventually, you'll discard them because they don't feel right.

For your personal success, you need to create and use your own statements. Just as your sneakers will only fit you perfectly, your Powerful Personal Statements will fit too.

Just imagine all the changes you can make to improve your life. You can move faster, higher, be stronger, and get yourself in the zone more quickly. You can stay calm, strong, and confident at tournaments and matches. Hey, you can even create the best mental coach who is with you daily-helping you to do your best!
Read on and you'll learn how you can easily create the statements which always work for you.

Powerful Personal Statements are only part of the process to help you achieve success.

There is still more to do. Luckily, it doesn't take a lot of time or energy to do the mental exercises necessary to achieve your personal goals, whether they are to increase your strength, confidence, speed, optimism, motivation, focus, self-discipline, resiliency, or improve your leadership qualities.

Chapter 8

Powerful Personal Statements - Success Starts Here

A carefully worded and well-formed personal statement is the key to aligning your thoughts and feelings with your desires and goals. A Powerful Personal Statement is simply a thought that you will use frequently to intentionally improve your sport and life.

You will be repeating your personal statement to help you stay on track and achieve your goal. A custom, well-thought-out statement will enable you to create new thoughts, beliefs, and behaviors to help you reach your goals without struggling.

In the upcoming chapters, you'll learn how to use your personal statement to easily stay on target and keep you focused on a specific outcome. Focusing on your outcome will eliminate the strain and stress which results from noticing those familiar worries and negative outcomes. Focusing on what you want will ultimately help you to enjoy the journey while you are reaching your goal.

This process has many names; focusing, mental imagery, mental rehearsal, visualization, and self-hypnosis. You'll be pleased to learn you only need between three and five minutes a few times a day to mentally practice to achieve success.

In the Appendix of this book, you'll find your personal worksheets. I suggest you take the time to complete your worksheets to clarify your goals and thoughts. (It only takes a few minutes.) Once you complete them, you can begin to integrate what you've learned and you'll start to notice if you are faced with personal resistance. By-the-way, there is nothing wrong or bad about resistance. It's simply information for you. Your worksheets will help you to create powerful statements which are specific to you, so you can reach any goal while feeling great and more optimistic.

As a National Guild of Hypnotists Certified Instructor, I teach the process of writing Powerful Personal Statements to all my students. As a Sports Recovery Hypnotherapist, I teach athletes step-by-step how to use their powerful statements every day to help them achieve their personal and professional goals.

It's important each client reinforces the thought and habit changes they desire, or they risk slipping back into old, unwanted patterns. Clients don't have to do this for months (or years). Reinforcement and repetition is only needed until those new thoughts, beliefs, and habits are in alignment with their goals.

When clients come to me for the first time, they learn what I do to help them doesn't come in the form of a "magic pill" (though it does sometimes seem magic). Clients learn that reinforcement and practice using Powerful Personal Statements is the key component to personal thought change and success. This requires practice and training, just as you practice and train your body.

As you learn and incorporate Powerful Thinking on Purpose into your life, you may notice how quickly it becomes second nature to you. You'll automatically begin to be more aware of your thoughts and easily remember to reinforce new habits and belief changes by repeating your personal statement.

Choose To Have A Great Day

What you think about and what you focus on is what you attract in your life.

If you discover only one thing from reading this book, the statement above is an important concept. You always have a choice about which thoughts you pay attention to. You can continue to think about "what is" (i.e. I'm never going to get better) or "what if", or you can choose to think about what you want and how you want to live your life.

MORNING EXERCISE

When you wake up in the morning and grumble about how frustrated you are and how everything takes too long, you are setting yourself up to feel frustrated for the rest of your day.

When you wake up in the morning and decide

I choose to have a great day today

then you have a much better chance of having a great day. Using your thoughts in a purposeful way will get you where you want to go.

Here's an easy way to show yourself your thoughts have power. Every morning for the next 14 days, as soon as you wake up, tell yourself you like the idea you have a great day. Repeat the following sentence in your mind or out loud 10 times each morning:

I like the idea I have a great day today

Then take a moment and imagine yourself at the end of the day smiling and feeling wonderful. It's OK if you don't believe you'll feel any better. Just give it a try. I guarantee the more you do this, the more you'll notice you feel much more positive when you check in with yourself at the end of the day.

In a short time, you will most likely notice a difference in your life. Perhaps something amazing has happened. Maybe something you didn't expect. Or maybe you notice your outlook or attitude has improved. With just this one exercise, you can jump-start yourself on the path to achieving your goals.

Nothing you are learning right now has to do with hoping or wishing. Every concept in this book is based on the science of how your subconscious mind works. Each of my clients learns the science of the mind during their first sessions. It's fascinating and easy to understand information. I frequently hear, "I wish I learned this in school!"

The most important and valuable skill you can develop in your life is the skill of intentionally directing your thoughts. Throughout the day you have thousands of thoughts. You already know persistent thoughts of worry, anxiety, and fear will always cause undue stress.

Replace Those Old Thoughts

Your new goal is to notice when you are having negative thoughts and ask yourself

How do I want to feel right now?

Then quickly change that thought to

"I like the idea I feel fine right now,"
or
"I like the idea everything works out and I feel great."

By noticing a negative thought or worry and quickly making a game of replacing it with the "I like the idea" sentence, you automatically feel more optimistic as your thoughts and feelings begin to focus on how you want to feel.

Chapter 9

Staying Calm in an Uncertain World

According to Dr. Andrew Weil, stress can cause a multitude of problems. On his web site Dr. Weil outlines some staggering facts about how stress can affect our lives:

1. Stress has been linked to all the leading causes of death, such as cardiovascular disease, cancer, and suicide.
2. Almost 90 percent of all visits to primary health care providers are due to stress-related problems.
3. Nearly one-half of all adults suffer adverse effects from stress.

It is estimated over one million Americans miss work due to stress-related complaints.

All of the above is true for athletes too.
Unfortunately anxiety and stress can also lead to increased risk of injury and reinjury.

Learning to change the way you talk to yourself in the midst of stressful situations can help you stay healthy and remain calm.

When I was pregnant with my first child, I found myself extremely stressed every time I watched the news because I now had another life to care for. Knowing I was going to be responsible for my child and realizing I had no control over what was going on in the world caused a huge amount of my stress.

At the time the Gulf War was in full swing. There was a frightening measles outbreak in the city. We were expecting the worst winter of the decade. Taxes were going up. The economy and our infrastructure needed major repairs. Our health system was a mess. Sound familiar? These were the headlines in 1989.

Not much has changed. Unfortunately, these are the same headlines which have bombarded us for decades.

I spent way too much time worrying and stressing about things had no control over.

Do you ever worry about things you have no control over? If you don't, then skip to the next chapter. If you do, I'm going to share a simple way to reduce your worry. First, consider this fact:

It's common to worry about something bad which might happen. Many of these worries start with "what if." During the time you worry, you are automatically causing yourself undue stress. When whatever it is you are worrying about doesn't happen, you will have spent a lot of time feeling stressed. Even if it does happen, you still will have spent a lot of time feeling stressed. Pretty much a no-win situation.

NOW YOU KNOW

A fear or worry is a thought about something which hasn't happened.

Wouldn't it be great if worrying could cause something wonderful to happen? It's a shame life doesn't work this way, especially because we spend so much energy and time worrying. But worrying never changes anything. Only action results in a change.

If stress and worry are useful feelings that cause you to take positive action, that's a good thing. Once you take the action you need, is continued worrying necessary?

For example, if you are going on a two-hour ride and you worry you'll run out of gas, you can take action. You can fill up your car with gas. Now you've taken action, the worry disappears.

If you are not in a position to take action, then what will worry do for you? Worrying without action is simply a waste of your good energy which can be used in a more helpful way.

Below are some typical issues we tend to worry about. Underneath each thought is a sample sentence you can say to yourself every time you catch yourself worrying.

After you begin substituting your new sentence, you'll start to notice how much better you feel. The better you feel, the more you'll want to incorporate these new sentences and thoughts into your everyday thinking.

TEST THIS ON YOURSELF: The moment you notice you are worrying or anxious, immediately:

1. Pretend or imagine you are releasing the thought. (Let it float away, or swipe it left, or erase it...any way you do this is OK.)

2. Ask yourself, "How do I want to feel?"
3. Then start your new positive sentence with the words: I like the idea that...

EXAMPLES

I'm worried I'll never get better.
I like the idea I heal easily.

I'm worried I'll make a mistake.
I like the idea I play a great game today.

I'm worried the economy will get worse.
I like the idea I'm financially secure and everything works out OK.

I'm worried I'll get injured again.
I like the idea my body is safe, strong, and healthy.

I'm worried I'll lose focus.
I like the idea it's easy for me to stay focused.

I'm worried I'll choke and lose.
I like the idea I stay calm and confident and play great today.

The phrase, ***I like the idea that***
will AUTOMATICALLY force you to:

1. Focus on *what you want* and
2. Reduce your stress

The more you use this phrase, the better you'll feel. It's amazing what the 5 Powerful Words, I like the idea that, can do.

I often use this technique during the day. Especially after I read the news. It's easy and effective.

Take a moment to do the following short exercise to show yourself how easy it is to feel better when you change your self-talk.

QUICK EXERCISE

1. Ask yourself, "What is my biggest worry right now?"
Example: "I am worried I won't perform well today."
Fill in the blank with your worry, anxiety, or fear:

I am worried that_____.

Read the above sentence and circle the possibility of that occurring.

0% - - - - - - 25% - - - - - - 50% - - - - - - %100
Not Possible ----------------------------------- Possible

I believe that there is a_____% chance of this occurring.

2.   Now write the opposite of your worry statement below:

Example: "I know I can perform at the top of my game today."

Fill in the blank with the outcome you want:

I _____.

Read the above sentence and circle the possibility of that occurring.

0% - - - - - - 25% - - - - - - 50% - - - - - - %100
Not Possible ----------------------------------- Possible

I believe that there is a_____% chance of this occurring.

87

Did you notice that both sentences you wrote, whether positive or negative, or worry, or desire, stated something that is possible?

It's interesting that most of the time, we tend to focus on the *negative* thought, even when there is *the possibility the outcome can be good too.*

Which thought feels better to you? The negative thought or the positive thought?

REWRITE your positive thought below:

I am_____.

Ask yourself: "How much do I believe this?"

If you don't believe your positive thought 100 percent,
then rewrite it here:

I like the idea that_____.

Ask yourself: "How much do I believe this thought now?"

By adding the five words, "I like the idea that," you have increased your belief in this thought. It is now a believable thought.

24 HOUR EXERCISE

Now that you have completed this simple exercise, you can see how easy it is to create a new, believable, powerful statement. For the next twenty-four hours, take the time to intentionally notice your thoughts. When they are heading into old negative territory take action:

Ask yourself: "How do I want to feel?"

Then quickly start your next thought with the outcome you desire:

I like the idea_____

You'll be pleasantly surprised when you find you have easily and automatically reduced your stress with this simple exercise.

REMEMBER:

A worry, anxiety, or fear, is a thought about the future.

Imagining the outcome you want is ALSO a thought about the future too.

Any time you notice the worry,
quickly reach for the thought that feels better.

NOW YOU KNOW

A well-formed Powerful Personal Statement is an effective tool you use to feel good about things you have no control over or when you want to reach a personal goal without struggling.

Chapter 10

How Does Powerful Thinking on Purpose Work?

According to hundreds of research studies, visualization techniques can improve motor skills, grow muscle strength, increase self-confidence, attention, concentration, and decrease anxiety.

You can harness the power of your mind through imagery to increase your motivation, your endurance, and even improve your performance.

Good to know, isn't it?

But how do you do that? Have patience future powerful thinker, because you are still learning!

When you are stuck with old thoughts which hold you back, it's almost impossible to take the action you need to achieve your goals.

Powerful Personal Statements are thoughts you *choose on purpose* which are designed to take root directly in your subconscious mind. Remember your subconscious mind is the one in charge of your emotions and feelings. You now get to instruct your inner mind on exactly what you want.

When a correctly worded powerful thought is accepted into your subconscious mind a new belief begins to form. This new belief then directly affects your attitude and, of course, ultimately your actions. As your attitude changes and you become open to possibilities, it then becomes easy to create the mindset you need while you practice or do your sport.

When you repeat and internalize your Powerful Personal Statement, you are actively creating positive changes in your subconscious mind. You have the ability to use your powerful statements to reprogram your mind, eliminate old emotional triggers, and respond to situations in a different way.

One way to understand this is your thoughts have a direct effect on your beliefs.

Your beliefs affect your attitude.
And your attitude has a direct effect on your actions.

THOUGHTS ➜ BELIEF
BELIEF ➜ ATTITUDE
ATTITUDE ➜ ACTION

Taking action is necessary for life changes to occur. Without action, nothing happens. Without action, everything remains the same.

Think of it this way. Without practice, you never get better. Without practice, you always remain the same.

Another way to look at this is first you think. Your thoughts cause you to feel a particular way. Your feelings affect what you do in your life. And what you do directly corresponds to what happens in your life.

"The ancestor of every action is a thought."
-Ralph Waldo Emerson

Let's say, for example, you want to improve your free throw percentage in basketball or putt more accurately in golf.

Unfortunately, every time you set up, your mind fills with negative chatter.

What if I miss?
This is too hard.
I'm worried I'm gonna choke again.

Everyone depends on me.
I hate that all eyes are on me.

How the heck do you silence that negative voice inside your head?

The first step to silencing old nagging negative voices is to notice these are simply thoughts about the future. And, unless you are psychic, you have no idea what the future is, do you?

Remember, these are simply thoughts. In the past, you paid attention to them, sometimes believing they were real. Most of the time, though, you were telling yourself you DID NOT want anything bad to happen. You knew you were holding a thought which represented the outcome you didn't want. But the more attention it got, the stronger it became. And then, of course, because your thoughts affect your actions, your subconscious got the message about the outcome you didn't want, and then...you blew it.

Happens all the time.

Luckily, there is an easy way to replace old negative thoughts with a powerful thought of the outcome you want.

It's just as easy as swiping a picture on your phone or changing a channel on a tv. If you are looking at photos on your phone, and you don't like one, you simply swipe it and another takes its place. If you don't like what's on tv, you pick up your remote and change the channel. This is the same thing my visually oriented clients do with their thoughts.

Scientifically, your mind can only hold one thought at a time. When you change the image or thought, it automatically replaces the old one, just like on your phone.

Your new goal is to create new neural pathways in your mind to automatically change how you see, how you feel, and how your body responds.

NOTE: If you are new at your sport and haven't practiced much, this technique will not magically make you become an expert!

The key to your success is to consistently practice your new way of thinking. When you combine it with proper visualization to feel calm and confident, you can easily hit the ball, make the shot, improve your performance, or increase your speed

QUICK EXERCISE:

Write a negative thought or worry below:

Examples:
"What if I miss?"
"This is too hard."
"I'm worried I'll make a mistake."
"I'm concerned I'll disappoint my teammates."
"I hate that all eyes are on me."
"I'm worried I'm gonna choke again."

Negative thought: _____
_____
_____

Write the outcome you want here: _____
_____
_____

Now look at the first sentence and say it a few times in your mind.

Does it feel true and believable? Sure, it's true and believable, because it's a pretty familiar thought isn't it?

Now, look at the second sentence - the outcome you want.

Repeat it in your mind a few times. Is your outcome sentence congruent with your thoughts and feelings? Does it feel true and right for you? When your sentence doesn't feel true, there is no way you can use it to help you reach a goal.

Maybe you noticed a little negative voice in the back of your mind saying "no…that won't happen,", or "I can't do it," or maybe feel as if you are making it all up.

In my experience, only a small percentage of people will find the outcome thought is completely 100 percent believable. Most people probably won't fully believe it. If you are in the latter group, you might notice something doesn't feel quite right about that sentence. Even though you'd like it to be absolutely true!

Perhaps you feel as if you are lying to yourself when you repeat the sentence. Not a big lie. Just a little one. The more you think about it, you know deep inside of you that statement doesn't ring true.

When you are trying to be positive and you don't fully believe what you are saying to yourself, those pesky negative thoughts will always pop right back into your head.

For a sentence to work for you, it must be congruent with your personal beliefs. It must feel right for you. When it is, it will become your Powerful Personal Statement.

If your subconscious mind (where your beliefs reside) does not accept this sentence, then you are wasting your time. Your willpower will run out and you'll give up quickly because it's too stressful to continually lie to yourself—no matter how much you want it to be true.

NOW YOU KNOW

When a correctly worded Powerful Personal Statement is accepted into your subconscious mind, it becomes a thought which is believable.

Your new believable thought will affect your attitude. Your attitude has a direct affect upon your actions. Your subconscious then makes sure your actions are in line with your thoughts.

This is why it's extremely important to hold the thought of the outcome you want.

Of course, simply reading or repeating a positive statement will not cause you to take immediate action. It is, however, the first step toward helping yourself create a new, beneficial belief in your subconscious mind.

When you use your Powerful Personal Statement, you aren't going to be simply repeating words to yourself. Nor will you be sitting quietly and hoping you'll succeed. You'll be "kicking it up a few notches" by combining your personal statement with some secret power ingredients which you'll learn later on in the book.

I Really Want This!

You can want something and at the same time not believe it's possible for you to achieve. This is the same as wishing and hoping.

There is a huge difference between wanting something and feeling, imagining, and knowing it is possible to attain.

Let's explore this concept.

Maybe you really want to make a lot of money.

Maybe you want to heal quickly and get back into the game.

Perhaps you want to improve your performance.

TAKE A MOMENT FOR YOURSELF NOW:

Write down a few things you want. Maybe you want more money. Maybe you want to be faster or stronger.

It might be, "I want to be the best player on my team this year," or "I want to heal quickly."

1. I really want_____.

2. I really want_____.

3. I really want_____.

After you have filled in the spaces above, rewrite #1 in the space below. Now, out loud, read the sentence below emphasizing the word "really."

"I _really_ want _____."

Now, say that sentence out loud five more times. Notice your thoughts and feelings while you repeat those words, then ask yourself

*Do I believe 100 percent to my very core I CAN
ACHIEVE THIS?*

Make sure your answer to this question is a simple
"Yes" or "No." Put your attention on your thoughts
and feelings while you answer the question.

Next, read the second sentence and ask yourself

*Do I believe 100 percent to my very core I CAN
ACHIEVE THIS?*

Finally, read the third sentence and ask yourself

*Do I believe 100 percent to my very core I CAN
ACHIEVE THIS?*

Yeah, But...

What were your thoughts and feelings when you answered these questions? Did you answer with a resounding "Yes!" If you did, it's proof your desires are congruent with your beliefs.

While answering the question above though, you may have noticed some internal thoughts and feelings. Perhaps you had a fleeting thought when you asked yourself if you believed you could achieve that. Or you might have noticed a small feeling which sounds like

"yeah, but..."

On the next page you will discover how to listen to yourself to identify any blocks which may get in the way of achieving your goals and desires.

INSTRUCTIONS:

If you had a *"yeah, but..."* feeling, say the sentence five times and <u>immediately jot down whatever comes to your mind</u> after the word "but."

Whatever pops into your head goes on the lines below. Place no judgments on your thoughts. It doesn't matter if your thoughts feel odd, ridiculous, or silly.

I really want _____
        (write your desired outcome above)

Quickly write your responses below.

     But_____

     But_____

     But_____

     But_____

What did you notice? What thoughts came to your mind after the word *"But"*?

Some people's sentences might look like this:

I want to be more consistent **but**…. <u>I don't believe it will really happen.</u>

I want to be more focused, **but**…. <u>It's really hard.</u>

I want to be in 100%, **but**…. <u>I'm worried I'll hurt myself</u>

I want to get on the team, **but**…. <u>I worry I won't have what it takes when the time comes.</u>

I want to be the best **but**…. <u>I've never been the best at anything.</u>

All of the above are examples of limiting thoughts and beliefs.

These are negative thoughts and beliefs which are huge mountains blocking and limiting your path to your goals. Because of this, they are commonly labeled "limiting beliefs" or "limiting thoughts."

NOW YOU KNOW

For a Powerful Personal Statement to work for you, it must feel TRUE for you. If it is not true you must add "I like the idea that..." so you can believe your thought.

Chapter 11
Getting Stuck by Limiting Beliefs

You hold two different types of beliefs in your subconscious mind. One kind of belief can stop you from moving forward, while the other belief can empower you to reach amazing heights.

A "limiting belief" is a thought in your mind which can get in the way of you moving forward in your life and achieving your goals. It's a thought which may have been true for you at one time, but may not be true now, even though part of your mind still acts as though it's relevant. There is nothing wrong with you. Everyone has them.

Of course, it's not your conscious analytical mind which holds this belief. Limiting beliefs are always firmly planted somewhere in your subconscious mind. Limiting beliefs can cause you to struggle while you attempt to reach your goal. Your subconscious wants to make sure what it believes and what you do are in alignment. When you want to achieve a goal and your subconscious doesn't believe it's possible, it will do its best to sabotage your success.

You might not know there is a limiting belief somewhere in the back of your mind, but you might notice a *"yeah, but..."* feeling inside yourself.

When you happen to notice a limiting belief and it's in the tiniest little voice you hear for only a moment, pay attention to it! Don't sweep it under the rug and hope it goes away. Your limiting belief is making itself known to you. This is a very valuable piece of information that can help you succeed in reaching your goals.

Limiting beliefs are a sign of personal inner subconscious resistance. You must address your own limiting belief in order to achieve success more easily. If you ignore it, it will cause you to constantly struggle and feel stressed while you are trying to reach your goal.

Below are examples of limiting beliefs:

I'm not good enough.

Other people are better than me.

It's selfish of me to want more.

To be successful I have to give up my personal and family life.

I'll never be fast, strong, or focused enough.

It takes too much time to practice.

Money is the root of all evil.

People who make a lot of money are snobs.

If I make a lot of money, my friends will be jealous.

"*What we can or cannot do, what we consider possible or impossible, is rarely a function of our true capability. It is more likely a function of our beliefs about who we are.*"

-Anthony Robbins

TAKE A MOMENT FOR YOURSELF:

No matter how uncomfortable or silly your beliefs may seem, it's important to pay attention to them because limiting beliefs will always get in the way of your success. If you ignore them, you'll find yourself struggling to stay on your path. When you pay attention to them, you have the opportunity to transform or release them.

Take a moment to jot down the first thoughts which come into mind when you read the following:

I'll never be good enough because

_____

_____

_____

I'll never be as successful as I want because

_____

_____

_____

The sentences you wrote above reveal you have limiting beliefs getting in the way of your success. Do others have limiting beliefs? Of course, everyone has beliefs and thoughts which can hinder their personal success.

Knowing limiting beliefs exist is a good start, but you are going further. You choose to be successful and do what you need to overcome them by taking control of your thoughts.

The big secret to personal success is recognizing and eliminating or changing these thoughts; when you do, you'll be well on your way to creating the mindset needed to achieve success.

Knowing you have thoughts that have been barriers on the path to your success is extremely useful information. Understanding this means you can now work towards eliminating these thoughts.

You are now learning to use Powerful Personal Statements to bypass and overcome these old limiting beliefs. At the same time, your new Powerful Personal Statement will smooth the path for your inner mind to accept your new positive beliefs.

By the way, there are other ways to effectively overcome past resistance and achieve your goals. You can pray, work with a therapist, tap on meridian points, and a myriad of other techniques. Some of those take a long time. I prefer to do things quickly and efficiently.

You can use your powerful statements alone or combine them with other techniques which are helpful to you. In my experience, using Powerful Personal Statements is simply the easiest, most cost-effective, and logical way to shift your thoughts, beliefs, attitudes, and ultimately your personal actions.

"Everything you want is out there waiting for you to ask. Everything you want also wants you. But you have to take action to get it."

-Jack Canfield

Many people like the idea that hoping and wishing for what they want will be enough to reach their goals. If only this were true! This would be an easy way to get what we want. When you hope and wish, all you get is more hoping and wishing. Of course, you now know this.

NOW YOU KNOW

Old beliefs can prevent you from achieving your goals

SUCCESS STORY

Michael Phelps is the most decorated Olympian in history with a record 28 medals. Once he developed his skills, he broke world records and forged an unrivaled career. It's no surprise he became the greatest American swimmer of all time because he trained not only his body, he committed to focusing on his mindset.

Wanting to be the best was the goal, but just wanting doesn't mean he would achieve it

Michael Phelps diligently used the power of his subconscious mind by imagining the cold water on his skin, the feeling of his goggles on his face, and most important - the end result. Utilizing the power of subconscious mental imagery at a deep level, he practiced the exhilarating feeling of winning each Olympic Gold Medal.

It's not enough to simply "THINK" about winning. It's *imperative* you pretend to imagine how you will feel, look, and sound. Using all your senses when you visualize or imagine is key to your success.

Chapter 12

Willpower Loses Again

Most people, when they want to make a change in their lives, tend to do it the hard way—by using all the willpower they can muster.

Imagine I'm placing a 2 x 4 wooden board on the ground. Now I ask you to balance and walk carefully with one foot in front of the other down the length of the board. You look at the board and of course, you know it's easy to do, so you confidently walk from one end to the other.

Now I'm going to take the same 2 x 4 board and raise it 4 feet off the ground. Now when I ask you to walk the length of the board from one end to the other, you feel nervous - your subconscious mind might shout, "NO!"

You were able to do it successfully when it was on the ground but now it's 4 feet above the ground, it is scary to walk the length of the board.

Your subconscious mind is now quite nervous and wondering whether you'll be safe. Will you be able to walk steadily on the board and avoid falling?

You might feel there is no way you can walk on the board and keep yourself safe. You'd have to use every ounce of willpower you can muster, but no amount of willpower is going to help you feel safe. The only way you can be successful is if your subconscious stays confident and calm.

Since raising the wooden board 4 feet off the ground makes you feel anxious and nervous, you now have a choice. You can choose to use your imagination to help you walk calmly across the plank of wood, or you can choose to try to walk while you are panicking and sweating.

You look at the high board and shake your head "no". It's not worth trying to use your willpower and stressing yourself to walk on the board. Willpower just lost - again.

When you stay confident and calm in your subconscious mind, it's not a problem…just look at any gymnast on a balance beam.

YOUR SUBCONSCIOUS MIND ALWAYS WINS

Using your imagination (located in your subconscious mind) rather than your willpower (located in your conscious mind) is the secret to achieving your goal without struggling.

Whcn you use your conscious mind, you want to be in control, but you probably won't believe you can. When you use your imagination, it's easy to pretend or imagine how it will feel to choose to be in total control.

In life you have many choices. You can choose to push through your fears with all the energy you can muster, or you can find a way to overcome them. You can choose to struggle, or you can choose to use Powerful Thinking on Purpose to help you reach your goals more easily. You are now learning how to take the struggle out of changes you desire in your life.

Your subconscious mind holds all of your emotions and given the choice between logic and emotion, emotions tend to win. Your imagination is the key to your happiness in life. Remember your subconscious mind holds the most powerful part of you: your imagination.

Imagine Your Success

Think back to a time in your life when you achieved a goal and felt proud of yourself. Perhaps it was when you rode your bike without training wheels for the first time. Maybe it was the time you tried out for a team, started a business, or got hired after a successful interview. What were your thoughts before you began? What were your thoughts throughout the process? What were your thoughts afterward?

Let's peek into the life of Tyler, a Junior who has been playing on the varsity baseball team since his Freshman year. He's a great team player. He's fast and confident. His coach and his teammates know he's headed for greatness..

Tyler has heard through the grapevine that college scouts will soon visit his school to watch him in action. Just the thought of a scout watching makes him nervous.
His heart starts to pound, his anxiety rises and he worries he's going to make a mistake and ruin his chances to get on a good team.

Every time he thinks about playing when scouts watch, he gets nervous. He worries his nerves will affect his game so much he'll never achieve his dream.

What kind of effect will these thoughts have on his game? The more he thinks this way, the more he sends a message to his subconscious - a message which indicates the outcome he doesn't want.

"I don't want to make a mistake."
"I don't want to look weak."
"I don't want to miss a shot."

Remember the subconscious doesn't recognize the word "don't"? Here's how his mind interprets those thoughts:

"I make mistakes."
"I look weak."
"I miss shots."

Tyler's thoughts will continue to repeat and drag him down. It's no surprise his constant worries about failure will affect his game. As a result of feeling bombarded with negative self-talk, Tyler is sending messages he doesn't want over and over to his subconscious.

These messages will cause Tyler to have to work hard to keep himself focused and play his best game. He'll use a lot of willpower fighting the worries about scouts watching, and making mistakes. That's a lot of energy that would be better spent playing his best game, isn't it? What do you think will happen when that willpower runs out?

If Tyler doesn't do something about his thoughts and mindset, he's going to lose the future he's worked so hard for.

"Imagination is everything. It is the preview of life's coming attractions."
-Albert Einstein

Chapter 13
Your Personal Protector

One of the functions of a healthy subconscious mind is to protect you. Your mind protects you from doing things that can cause you physical or emotional pain. You learned early on touching fire will result in a painful burn. This knowledge is firmly and permanently implanted in your mind and prevents you from placing your hand on a hot stove.

Throughout your life you've kept yourself safe and probably have never walked in the middle of a fast-moving highway. You've never put your life at risk by swimming in a lagoon populated with hungry alligators either. You keep yourself safe and don't consciously put yourself in situations where you can get hurt.

Your subconscious mind also protects you from engaging in activities that might cause you to fail. For example, if you are aware you are an average skier, you won't take the risk of hurting or embarrassing yourself by attempting to ski on the expert trails.

Your subconscious mind also protects you from creating personal inner conflicts. So if you believe rich people are snobby and shallow, then you'll protect yourself from becoming successful and rich because you don't want to be considered snobby and shallow.

Our Minds Are Open When We Are Young

When we are young, we are learning how things work in the world This is the time when we soak in everything around us. As babies and as children, we absorb information from the moment we are awake until the second we drift into sleep. We hear and learn from our parents, teachers, clergy, siblings, friends, TV, internet, movies, and radio.

It's no surprise when we were young, we believed most of what we saw and heard. This is because young children don't have the same internal filters and judgment which adults have acquired.

Children do not usually analyze what they notice around them. They don't ask themselves, "Is this something helpful for me to believe?" They don't intentionally choose to accept or reject a particular thought; they simply allow new thoughts to form, without question.

You already know one of the most common fears among adults is the fear of public speaking. Some people get so nervous and anxious when speaking in front of groups they will do anything to get out of the situation.

Think of this scene. A mother and her seven-year-old daughter Abby are getting ready to leave their house for the day. The mother is packing up her briefcase and she's talking to herself about how much she hates having to give the annual presentation at work. She's clearly nervous, and would prefer to avoid the situation.

Abby has been quietly playing and listening to her Mom's grumbling.

Can you imagine any seven-year-old saying this to her mother?

"Gee Mom, I understand you have unresolved issues and complex anxieties about speaking in public, and while you choose to continue believing you can never speak comfortably in front of others, I have decided this is your internal issue. I choose not to develop the same fear you have developed."

An adult might respond this way, but never a young child.

A more likely scenario is the daughter remains silent while she listens to her mom. She may begin to hold the belief there is something frightening about speaking in public because she saw how nervous and upset her mom would get. She might grow up thinking it is normal to be anxious when speaking to groups. Because Abby has never given a presentation or felt nervous, she might never remember where her fear came from.

Everything a child hears, notices, and experiences can pass directly into their subconscious mind, without question. As a result, we all tend to form opinions and beliefs based on our unfiltered experiences which can ultimately create limiting beliefs later in our lives.

Thankfully, with age and experience, your conscious mind has the maturity and the ability to question long-held beliefs.

As we get older, we don't automatically believe everything we are told. For example, if you meet your new next-door neighbor and she says "My son is the best basketball player in the US," would you believe her? Of course not.

However, if this same neighbor tells your five-year-old-niece she is the mom of the top basketball player in the country, would your niece believe her?

Your niece might believe her without question because, in her limited experience, all adults tell the truth. At the tender age of five, she hasn't created the filters in her mind that adults have learned to rely on. As young children, we tend to believe what we see and hear as truth.

When we are children, we are rarely aware our subconscious mind has been exposed to other people's worries and beliefs. When we are young, we often internalize others' beliefs and worries unwittingly. These internalized worries and beliefs can cause us personal struggles later in life. When this happens, we are at risk of experiencing life through other people's filters rather than our own.

Michael

Michael is in 4th grade and loves playing soccer after school. His friends play too, and he looks forward to being outside and kicking the soccer ball around. It's his favorite thing to do. He even practices in his back yard after school when the weather is good. His mom picks him up when practice is over.

On a Saturday, while playing against another team, Michael sees the ball coming right at him. He quickly runs up to kick that ball right into the goal!

SCORE! "I did great!" he thinks to himself, grinning ear to ear.

A second later he notices the silence. No one cheers. He hears laughter. In the background, he hears his coach say, "I can't believe he did that. He is the weakest player on the team."

Oh no. He turns around to see what happened. He can't believe what just happened. He kicked the ball into his team's net! He scored for the other team! As he walks off the field he hears his teammates laughing and boo-ing...he feels so ashamed.

At home that evening he is in the other room when his mom tells his dad about the game. Dad laughs and says, "I was never good at sports when I was his age. I tried really hard I made too many mistakes because I couldn't focus. No one in our family is good at sports.

Michael has heard him say things like this before. He's never questioned it. It's simply something he's overheard throughout his young life. "I tried hard to do well in sports, but never could. People in our family aren't good at sports."

The reality is when Michael hears his Dad repeatedly talk about how people in the family just arcn't good at sports, he knows it's true - without question.

Internally, his subconscious decided

Gosh, if no one in our family does well in sports, I probably won't do well either. I love playing soccer but I'll never be good enough.

Remember Mark doesn't have the tools and judgment an adult has.

He won't think

Wow. Dad was never good at sports. Maybe he didn't enjoy them. While that's OK for Dad, I really love playing soccer. And how do I know it's true that no one in our family is good at sports? I know I am a different person than Dad. I'm only in 4th grade and it's OK to make mistakes. My teacher tells me "everyone can practice and improve." I'm going to practice and get better so I do well when I play.

He subconsciously accepts what his Dad said as truth. If his Dad wasn't good, and no one in his family was good, then it stands to reason that he'll never be any good at sports either.

And another limiting belief gets formed.

Red Alert! Limiting Belief Forming Ahead!

One day I was driving with my eight-year-old son in the car. We were chatting about friends and relatives when he said:

"Mom, I never want to be rich."

"Why do you say that?" I responded.

"Well, rich people are crazy," he said.

"What do you mean?" I questioned.

"Mr. Smithson is kind of crazy and he has lots of money. I don't want to be crazy when I grow up so I don't want to be rich like him," he explained.

I was surprised to hear this. I had no idea why or how he put these two thoughts together. Our neighbor, Mr. Smithson has an odd sense of humor, and likes to wear costumes on Halloween. But crazy? No. Hmm…I thought, this sounds like a belief that may limit him later in his life. I'd better say something to help clear up his misconceptions about money causing people to be "crazy."

For the next few minutes, we talked about rich people and how all people are different regardless of the amount of money they make.

I asked him to think of a Disney Channel actor who he thought might make a lot of money… After he named a person, I asked him if he thought the actor was crazy.

"No," he replied, "I think she would be nice, just like the person she plays on TV."

The thought that "all rich people are crazy" was at the risk of becoming a belief. By simply helping him realize that people are different, regardless of the money they have, I helped him to avoid this limiting belief taking root in his subconscious mind.

Every time we help a person to clear up a misconception, we are helping them to stop limiting beliefs from negatively affecting their lives.

"The mind is a dutiful servant and will follow the instructions we give it."
-Zig Ziglar

Chapter 14

Creating Effective Powerful Personal Statements

The key to Powerful Thinking on Purpose is to create powerful personal statements to help you feel better and be in control of your thoughts, beliefs, attitudes, actions, and habits.

In this chapter, you will learn how to form powerful personal statements which will always work for you. You'll be creating your own statements, custom designed by you, to propel yourself to success.

When you repeat your powerful personal statements every day, you can expect profound and measurable changes in how you feel and your outlook on life. Right now, the only things standing between you and your personal successes are your thoughts.

7 RULES FOR CREATING POWERFUL PERSONAL STATEMENTS

1. Your personal statement must <u>be framed in the present.</u>
2. Your personal statement must <u>be positive.</u>
3. Your personal statement must <u>be simple.</u>
4. Your personal statement must <u>be believable.</u>
5. Your personal statement must <u>have a reward.</u>
6. Your personal statement must <u>feel true for you.</u>
7. If it's not true for you, <u>include the 5 Powerful Words: "I like the idea that..."</u>

Keep reading and you'll learn how easy it is to create powerful personal statements to change your life.

RULE 1: YOUR PERSONAL STATEMENT MUST BE FRAMED IN THE PRESENT TENSE

Read the two sentences below:

1. I exercise every day and I feel great.
2. I will exercise every day and I will feel great.

Notice there is a subtle difference between the two sentences.

Sentence A) is correctly stated in the present tense.

Sentence B) contains the word "will."

Remember, your subconscious mind is very literal. What you say is what you get. Also, your subconscious mind has no opinion, though it is your personal protector. So when you say to yourself:

I *will* exercise every day and I *will* feel great

your subconscious mind will hear the sentence EXACTLY as it is written. The definition of the word "will" is "going toward." It means what you are thinking of doing is going to occur in the future but hasn't happened yet.

So your subconscious will interpret this to mean:

At some time in the future, I don't really know when, it could be tomorrow, it could be next week, it could be next year, I plan to exercise every day and I will feel great.

If your goal is to start now, rather than sometime in the future, then it's imperative you choose the correct words to describe your goal.

The preferred wording can be found in the statement below:

A) I exercise every day and I feel great.

This statement works because it sounds like it's already part of your daily work routine. It happens today, tomorrow, and every day.

When forming your powerful personal statement, two words that are important to avoid are HOPE and TRY.

The word "hope" means to desire something with the expectation it is likely to happen, but with the possibility it might not. When you focus on hoping something will happen, your subconscious frequently waffles back and forth between imagining it will happen and imagining it won't happen.

Hoping causes conflicting thoughts in your subconscious mind.

The definition of "try" is: To make an attempt or effort.

Because your subconscious mind takes words literally, this means if you "try" something, you are attempting something, not actually doing it. If you decide to try to bake a loaf of bread today what you are really saying is you are going to attempt to bake a loaf of bread.

Will you bake a loaf of bread today? Maybe you will or maybe you won't. But you might try.

When you say you will "try," you are NOT stating you will accomplish your task.

> *"Try not.*
> *Do, or do not.*
> *There is no try."*
> **-YODA**

Years ago, when my daughter was younger, I would remind her to clean her room.

She said, "I'll try to do it, Mom." And she did. Sometimes she cleaned her room, but often she didn't. When she was a teenager and understood what the word "try" meant, she often responded with "I'm doing my best!" (She quickly learned the power of language!)

TIP: Keep the words will, hope, and try out of your powerful personal statements.

RULE 2: YOUR PERSONAL STATEMENT MUST BE POSITIVE

Eliminate DON'T, WON'T, and other negative words. Remember the pink elephant?

RULE 3: YOUR PERSONAL STATEMENT MUST BE SIMPLE

Because you'll be repeating your powerful statement throughout the day, it's important to make sure it's simple. It's much easier to remember a simple sentence than a complex one. Read the two sets of examples below and decide which of the following sentences would be easier to repeat ten times daily.

EXAMPLE A

Every day I swim I stay focused on what every single muscle in my body is doing and always make sure my breath is perfect and I imagine my long muscles gliding strong and powerful, making sure I use all my energy every time I swim.

EXAMPLE B

Every time I swim I am strong, powerful and fast.

EXAMPLE A

Every time I ride in a horse show I always ignore others who are watching me and keep my attention on my horse and do what I know how to do so that he does what he needs to do and I remember to sit properly and stay calm and think about my posture.

EXAMPLE B

Every time I ride I am calm and confident.

EXAMPLE B is much easier to remember, isn't it? When your personal statement is easy to remember, you'll find it easier to repeat.

Some people find it fun to create personal statements that rhyme or sing them to the chorus of a favorite song. Feel free to do this as long as it remains simple. For example, if you wanted to exercise more, you might say, "Every time I run, I have a lot of fun."

Remember: Keep your powerful personal statements simple.

RULE 4: YOUR PERSONAL STATEMENT MUST BE BELIEVABLE

Simply put, this means your personal statement must be something you believe you can accomplish.

If you want to become the next Olympic power lifter and you can't lift more than 50 lbs, then most likely you have a long way to go before the end result will be believable.

However, it can be believable when you chunk your goal into smaller ones. For example, "I enjoy lifting weights every week," will start you on your journey to success.

It's important to set up outcomes for yourself which are believable. When we set up goals for ourselves that are too big or overwhelming, we tend to do one of two things: We either freeze and don't even bother to begin, or we start and quickly give up because we feel we'll never be able to reach our goal.

How many times you have made a New Year's resolution? How many of your resolutions lasted throughout the year?

It's no surprise the first quarter of the year is the most popular time for health clubs to gain new members. The fact is that 50 percent of all new health club members quit within the first six months of signing up. Most people join with the intention of exercising frequently. ("I'm going to exercise five days a week now that I've joined the gym.") They set their expectations so high that when they miss a few days, they feel they have failed. They have completely overwhelmed themselves with their commitment. Rather than start slowly and achieve small successes, they give up because their goal was too difficult.

When you break your goal down into smaller pieces, it is easier to achieve. It's easier to experience those small successes and feel good about yourself.

Let's say you decide to run a marathon. You are healthy and in great shape. You know you can push yourself, you are athletic and play tennis four times a week.

Here is the statement you decide to start with

Every day I run fifteen miles and I feel great.

Read it again and ask yourself the following questions:

Is this believable?
Can I even run that much right now?

Think about your answers. Be honest with yourself. If you haven't run for a while and you try for fifteen miles on your first day, you aren't likely to finish. When that happens you'll feel disappointed. And when you feel disappointed a part of you doesn't want to do it again. Feeling disappointed is never a good motivator.

Since you are just beginning, doesn't running 3 - 5 miles a day seem more believable than running fifteen? Sure it does. After you've easily run 5 miles each day, you can add more miles slowly. By the end of a few months you will have easily trained yourself to run more than you imagined.

If your stated goal doesn't feel believable, start small and add slowly. Even running one mile a day will get you to your success. Achieving each successive goal is the easy way to improve your performance. Small goals will help you enjoy running and enhance the personal motivation you need to run the marathon.

DON'T SHOULD ON YOURSELF

Most people tend to choose things they feel they "should" be doing. If you have a "should" thought inside, you need to change your statement.

A "should" sets you up for disappointment and failure because a "should" is frequently someone else's voice (or rule) inside of you. You didn't choose it.

When you choose something you WANT to do, it's far more easy to stay motivated and follow through.

A very wise person once told me, "DON'T SHOULD on yourself, and DON'T SHOULD on others."

Wise words indeed.

RULE 5: YOUR PERSONAL STATEMENT MUST HAVE A REWARD

I'm not talking about a reward such as a wad of cash or a new car. What I mean by a reward is there must be something positive and good you will achieve as a result of reaching your objectives and goals.

It's human nature to either want to do things that avoid pain or take action that results in feeling good. For example, when we go to work, we get a reward in the form of a paycheck. A paycheck is a good incentive to get up in the morning and go to work. It goes without saying most people would choose to stay home if they didn't receive their reward of money.

Another example of a reward is the one that happens when you set a goal and achieve it. The main reason for running is so you can enjoy the challenge, stay strong, work out, feel great, and enjoy improved health. These are wonderful rewards! Would you bother running if there were no benefits at all?

Here are some examples of rewards you can put at the end of your personal statement:

- I feel great.
- I feel safe.
- I am proud of myself.

EXAMPLES:

I like the idea it's easy to drink healthy beverages when I'm with friends and I am proud of myself!
I like the idea my body is strong and healthy and I am safe when I play!

Feeling good is the best motivator on the planet.

RULE 6: YOUR PERSONAL STATEMENT MUST FEEL TRUE FOR YOU

This is by far the most important rule. If this rule is ignored, repeating your personal statement is simply a waste of time. If your statement doesn't feel true for you, then it's no more effective than a bandaid on a fractured ankle.

Every personal statement you create must be tested in your mind to determine how it feels for you. This crucial step is necessary so your subconscious mind will accept your statement so you can achieve success.

This is your turning point. Ignore this rule and you'll never move forward. You'll continually be blocked by your subconscious mind which wants to protect you.
Always make sure your statement feels true for you - it will lead you to personal success.

One of my clients, Dave, had the goal of being relaxed and comfortable whenever he spoke in public. He knew being interviewed was something elite athletes experienced and when it happens to him, he didn't want to sound ignorant or stumble on his words. He had many friends who were calm and confident every time they spoke and it was time for him to stop holding himself back.

When he was in fourth grade, he was standing in front of the class ready to present his book report. He had fun playing the parts of the major characters as he told a story to his peers. They laughed and clapped in the appropriate places. He felt great!

A few years later, Dave had a life-changing experience.

In middle school, he was called on to answer a simple history question. He knew the answer but his mind went completely blank. He opened his mouth and a few syllables came out, but he couldn't get his thought out. His best friend knew Dave could answer almost any history question that was thrown at him but when he saw the blank look on Dave's face, he couldn't help himself and laughed out loud.

Fast forward to today and now when Dave speaks his body is full of nerves and anxiety. Before he speaks, he gets hot and sweaty, his heart pounds, and he panics imagining he will trip over words. He's able to finish his presentation, but it's extremely painful. He's experiencing a true fear: the very common fear of speaking in public.

Even though his conscious mind knows he won't die when he speaks, his subconscious mind screams at him in fear, worried something bad will happen or people will laugh and make fun of him. The thought of speaking triggers those old reactions which happened when Dave was younger.

To try to overcome his discomfort, Dave creates the following personal statement for himself:

I am comfortable whenever I speak in front of a group

As he repeats his statement, he hears a little voice inside say

Who are you kidding?
You know you panic and everyone will laugh at you

Earlier you learned your subconscious mind is designed to protect you. Its primary goal is to keep you safe. Dave's subconscious mind doesn't believe he will be safe when he speaks in front of a group. So his "helpful" subconscious mind sends Dave thoughts like "don't speak in front of others." Unfortunately, Dave's career requires speaking to groups monthly.

Dave is required to run the monthly team meetings. But, his subconscious mind is desperate for him to stop speaking. It sends him thoughts like "do it!" But Dave must talk, so he does his best to ignore those thoughts.

The only thing left now is for his protective subconscious to send Dave strong feelings to get him to stop. Every time Dave speaks in public, his body now is the recipient of those strong feelings: the sweats, and his heart pounding.

Dave decides to create a new positive statement to help himself when he speaks in public:

I like the idea that I am calm and confident every time I speak and I feel great.

As Dave repeats his new personal statement, he feels comfortable. It's a thought that feels good. He smiles and feels a bit optimistic. (He really does like this idea!)

Dave continues to repeat his personal statement for the next few weeks. The morning of his team presentation at work, he is pleased to notice he actually feels peaceful and relaxed. Dave repeats his statement a few times in his mind as he stands. He calmly delivers his presentation and sits down with a smile. He is thrilled he felt normal, calm, and relaxed. Soon after, he joins Toastmasters International to improve his presentation skills. Dave is quite the success story and now is actively involved in Toastmasters, helping others improve their speaking skills.

Megan's Powerful Personal Statement

Megan has been a gymnast since she was four. She has always excelled and scored well in competitions. Her coaches and teammates view her as fearless. A month ago she was in the gym practicing her backflip. At the beginning of her second flip she heard an unusual sound at the other side of the gym. She lost her focus, mistimed her flip, and landed with a thud.

She was embarrassed and shocked. Nothing like that had never happened to her. She stood up to begin again and her feet froze with fear. Her heart was pounding. She was terrified about attempting another backflip. With tears in her eyes, she walked out of the gym. She felt upset and out of control.

The next day Megan realizes she has to do something to overcome her fear. She can't let it take control. She has always done well with backflips but somehow, this one knocked the confidence right out of her.

She decides to create a Powerful Personal Statement for herself:

I successfully do my backflips and I feel great.!

Remembering what she learned about Powerful Thinking she knew she had to figure out if this felt true for her. She closed her eyes and took a few deep breaths.

In her mind, she repeated her sentence slowly, over and over. She took the time to go inward and put her attention on the words she was thinking. She noticed how her body felt. She noticed what images showed up. In a short time, she opened her eyes and shook her head. She knew her statement didn't feel 100% true to her. Her heart was pounding. She was scared of falling again. She was frightened she might truly hurt herself the next time.

She quickly changed her statement to

I like the idea I'm safe every time I do a backflip and I feel great!

While she repeated this new statement, she imagined herself in the future quickly doing backflips and finishing perfectly - with a big smile. She heard her coach say "good job!"

Before bed she took some time to imagine completing twenty successful backflips while repeating her sentence.

The next day her coach spotted her. She repeated her sentence, imagined she had completed it safely, and quickly executed a perfect backflip.

Jake's Powerful Personal Statement

Jake is a competitive swimmer and is ready to try out for the Olympic Team. He's got a lot going on in his life. A new baby at home. His mom is recovering from surgery, his family is moving to a new home and the list of tasks to complete keeps growing. It feels as if his whole life is turning upside down and there are days he feels overwhelmed.

He noticed the last few times he swam he was so stressed he executed his flip turns poorly.

He couldn't stop stressing about how his stress might affect his swimming.

He sits down and closes his eyes and lets his thoughts flow for a moment…
His big concern are his flip turns. He must get them under control. Jake knows the more he worries about them, the worse he'll perform.

He pretends to imagine himself swimming smoothly, quickly, and strongly and executing each turn effortlessly. He's done this before. It's hard-wired into his muscle memory.

He is aware that worry affects him every time he swims so he thinks to himself

"Every time I swim I don't stress or worry."

He lets this thought simmer in his mind...no, he thinks to himself...that's not right...I want to find the opposite of the words "stress" and "worry" because I don't want the thoughts of "stress" and "worry" in my mind.

Every time I swim I work hard and execute my flip turns perfectly.

Closing his eyes, he repeats the new thought and notices a subtle tension beginning to grow in his shoulders. He knows something about the sentence is causing tension. A thought bubbles up in his mind. He recalls his father complaining about how much he hates to work hard every day.

His father would grumble "I hate working," and drink too much on the days he opened the envelope containing his meager paycheck. OK, thought Jake, maybe I'm responding to the word "work".

Every time I swim my flip turns are perfect and I swim fast!

He sits down, closes his eyes, and repeats his positive statement five times. Ahh...that feels right. No tension. It's easy for me to repeat. I've executed my turns in the past. I can easily say those words. I really DO like that idea.

Was his Powerful Personal Statement true for him? Yes.

Anytime you say a personal statement and it doesn't feel true or right for you, you have smacked right into your own personal barrier. This barrier indicates there is something inside you—most likely an uncomfortable memory, erroneous thought, or a limiting belief—which can block you from achieving your success.

Remember, it's not intended to block you from your goal, rather it is your subconscious mind doing its job to PROTECT you from feeling bad in some way.

RULE 7: IF IT'S NOT TRUE FOR YOU, INCLUDE THE 5 POWERFUL WORDS

It's human nature to want to postpone tasks that don't offer an obvious reward for completion. A good example is doing taxes. Many people put their taxes off until the last moment. They don't feel excited to sit down, fill out paperwork, and then write checks. I don't mind paying taxes. I do feel grateful for the benefits we get from taxes but I just don't want to spend hours organizing and filling out paperwork.

I used to put my taxes off until the last few weeks. Even though I tried to ignore doing taxes, in reality, I caused myself undue stress because thoughts about my unpaid taxes still took up a lot of space in my mind. "I have to do my taxes today" went through my mind a couple of times each day from February through March.

This year I decided to reduce my stress and changed how I thought about doing my taxes by repeating this statement:

I easily and quickly complete my taxes and I feel great!

I looked at my personal statement and read it out loud. Of course, I liked the idea of completing something and feeling great.

The truth is, I knew it wasn't true. Total B.S. Never once did I ever complete them quickly.

I read it again and I noticed this statement made me feel like I was trying to force myself into believing something that wasn't true. The word "quickly" bothered me; it didn't even feel possible.

The first thing I did was to take out the word "quickly":

I easily complete my taxes before April and I feel great.

There was still something about my statement which still didn't feel 100 percent true. Maybe about 60 percent true. I had no clue why, but I knew I had hit a wall of resistance.

I knew if it wasn't true, I wouldn't achieve my stated goal. It was time to change my statement and preface it with the 5 Powerful Words:

I like the idea that...

Here was my new statement:

I like the idea that I easily complete my taxes before April and I feel great!

I read it again. I do like this idea! Once I mail my taxes, I know I'll stop thinking about them for at least another ten months. Getting them done and out of the way will definitely free my mind from the stress.

Adding the 5 Powerful Words shifted my personal statement from just 60 percent to <u>100 percent believable.</u>

After repeating my powerful personal statement for a week, I was surprised I wanted to finish my taxes and get them out of the way. This was definitely a new experience for me. For the first time, I finished and mailed them before February 1st. Done. Completing the paperwork felt great!

I Like The Idea That...

These 5 Powerful Words have the power to propel a positive statement instantly from 60 percent believable to 100 percent believable. They even have the ability to take your statement from 10 percent to 100 percent.

One benefit of adding these 5 Powerful Words is once your subconscious mind accepts your personal statement as true for you, things can rapidly begin to change.

Many people notice at some point they naturally stop using the 5 Powerful Words. They become aware they are now repeating their earlier, shorter statement. When this happens, its your personal indicator you have successfully internalized your powerful personal statement and now believe this to be true for you.

When your personal statement is TRUE FOR YOU, your subconscious mind can accept it as truth and allow you to reach your goal without being held back by old
limiting beliefs.

NOW YOU KNOW

Your 5 Powerful Words have the power to increase the strength of your personal statement quickly and effortlessly. You can think of it as a magic accelerant for your personal success.

Chapter 15
See, Feel, Hear, Repeat

WHAT YOU THINK ABOUT, YOU BRING ABOUT

After you have created your powerful personal statement, you need to add a few simple ingredients to the mix to make it work faster and easier. This is the fun part of Powerful Thinking on Purpose. Not only will you feel great in the moment, but you also get to focus your thoughts on what you want, which ultimately helps you reach your desired goal. You'll be doing this daily by using your powerful imagination.

What we think about, we attract to ourselves. Remember the concept of plants, flowers, and bushes in your garden attracting birds, butterflies, and insects? Your thoughts also attract things, feelings, and the ability to see opportunities and possibilities.

When you think negative thoughts, what happens? You start to feel bad, frustrated, unhappy, angry, or sad.

When you think positive thoughts, what happens? You can feel calm, relaxed, empowered, and excited.

Below are four important steps to help you feel and experience what it will be like to achieve success. In the process, you'll also get the bonus of feeling good.

SEE

The Widescreen TV Technique

Imagine right in front of you is a large flat screen TV. An image of you having already achieved your goal is right there on the screen in full, bright color. You might imagine yourself having finished at your personal best. You could see yourself in the future mentoring young people and sharing your successes. Maybe imagine walking and holding hands with your perfect partner talking about how grateful you are. Have fun with your imagination here. There are no limits!

Now, enlarge the image of you on the screen to make it life-size.

Next, pretend to step right into that image of you. It's as easy as putting on a costume. You put your feet in first, then your arms, and then your head.

You pull up the zipper and voila! You now ARE the new you!

Feel all the good feelings you can imagine as if you have achieved your goal. See yourself in your new body of success. Feel how good you feel. What do you see around you? Imagine feeling absolutely wonderful as you are doing a huge happy dance now that you have reached your goal - and knowing you can achieve anything you want!

NOTE: At this point, it's OK to pretend you are in your new body. You don't have to imagine it in full detail or color. Simply pretend it's happened.

HEAR

Now as you imagine yourself as this new, successful "you" in your TV, you must say your powerful personal statement.

Repeat it ten times while you are inside the successful you of the future. You can repeat it in your mind or out loud. Either way, you'll experience the same result. While you are repeating your statement, notice what it sounds like to be successful. Hear yourself repeating your personal statement while you are in your new body of success. Hear what you say to yourself. Hear what others say to you. Way to go! You rock!

FEEL

You can now maximize the power of your personal statement by adding positive feelings while you are imagining yourself in your success picture. While you are repeating your statement, you can pretend or imagine you have reached your goal. Feel how great it feels to be successful, you are a winner! You feel so proud of yourself! Keep on feeling these feelings and notice how great you feel inside.

Your success picture can be still or moving. How you imagine it is up to you. Some people like to imagine themselves doing something they enjoy, either alone or with friends and family. When you allow your creative mind to come up with fun and positive scenes, you'll find it's easy to want to put yourself in them even more often.

One fun way is to imagine yourself calling a friend and sharing how great you are feeling now that you have achieved your goal:

Guess what? I did it! I feel great!

Notice how good you feel when your friend says:

Wow. You are awesome. You did it. I'm proud of you!

Have fun with this scene. Make it feel even more amazing. Grow the scene til it becomes bigger than life. Make the colors big and bright. Double the feelings. Look at the smile on your face. You feel great. You look great. Notice all the sounds, sights, and feelings of this great big awesome scene!

REPEAT

Changing your subconscious thoughts using the techniques you've learned in this book is a great way for you to reduce your stress and achieve your goals.

If you come across a personal issue that seems to have many limiting beliefs and you feel overwhelmed, then consider seeking professional help, such as a coach or Certified Hypnotherapist.

Repeating your powerful personal statement will always help you feel better - every day. Every time you repeat it, you automatically create feelings of optimism, hopefulness, anticipation, enthusiasm, and happiness. In the moment, when you focus on something you want, you automatically send a wonderful positive feeling throughout your mind and body.

Remember when you first learned your sport? You practiced small movements until they became second nature. Then you practiced more as your body acclimated to your sport. Then you learned ways to improve and make the changes you needed to become great at what you do. You trained your mind and body through practice.

The key concept of training is also true for your thoughts. Just like your body holds muscle memory, your thoughts also hold patterns. To change those patterns you must re-train your mind and practice!

The more you intentionally create powerful thoughts on purpose, the more your mind automatically access them subconsciously. The more you focus on your powerful personal statements, the more positive thoughts you create. Imagine how much better you'll feel when positive thoughts become second nature to you.

TIP: For additional reinforcement and success, write your personal statement on a piece of paper several times a day. Every time you write, you can intentionally pretend to put yourself in the future place which feels good—as if you have already achieved success. The more you feel, hear, and see yourself as successful, the more this thought becomes integrated into your subconscious mind.

Say your powerful personal statements every day. Just like training, frequent practice is tremendously more effective than sporadic practice. When you practice consistently, you create a powerful compounding effect that helps your subconscious accept your positive statement much more quickly.

The best way to start your day is to repeat your personal statement ten times in the morning—before you put your feet on the floor. Repeat it ten times before you go to sleep. Another great time to repeat them is when you exercise or walk. Anytime you do something which doesn't require concentration, you can repeat your personal statement.

You cannot overdo reinforcement.

REMEMBER: See, Feel, Hear, Repeat

Chapter 16

You Didn't Learn This in School

Every day we have thousands of thoughts - anywhere from 14,000 to 57,000. Add this to the hundreds of daily decisions. What to wear, what to eat, where to go, what to read, what to tackle first, what sites to visit on the web, who to call, when to go, how to get there, etc.,

If you wrote every thought you had on a piece of paper, you might notice most of them are repetitive old thoughts. Many of them are worries, fears, and general negative thoughts.

Think of the dozens of "what if" thoughts that swirl in the mind, especially after hearing the news. It's easy to realize we do indeed have thousands of thoughts daily.

When you notice you are thinking about something you don't want, you can quickly change your thought to feel better and be in control of your actions.

Your awareness of your thoughts is the first step toward making a positive change to feel good and open the doors to new possibilities.

Remember, your thoughts affect your beliefs. Your beliefs directly affect your attitude, and your attitude directly affects your actions.

An easy way to determine if you are thinking about things you don't want is below:

**When you feel bad,
you are thinking about something you don't
want in your life.**

**When you feel good,
you are thinking about something you do
want.**

In Chapter 9, Staying Calm in an Uncertain World, you learned when you worry about something you cannot control, you can stop for a moment and think of positive outcome. You can use your imagination and make up any outcome you desire. Then add your 5 Powerful Words in front of your thought.

You Always Have a Choice

When I was growing up, our family went to visit my grandparents for a family dinner most weekends. I remember my father saying to me,

"You always have a choice, Wen. You can go to your grandparents' house and choose to be miserable, or you can go to your grandparents' house and choose to have a good time."

Even at age seven, I knew this was a no-brainer. I made the choice to enjoy myself while visiting my grandparents. It was that easy.

By the time I was a teen, I felt as if I had very few choices in my life. I couldn't choose to do what I wanted when I wanted. My parents put limits on me which were not my choice. ("What do you mean I have to be home by midnight?") As a young adult, I felt society was limiting me. As I got older, I felt as if I had fewer and fewer choices.

Many years later, David Crump, a brilliant man who created the Essential Experience Workshop, made a profound statement that changed my life. I was in the perfect place in my personal development to hear and incorporate his insight into all aspects of my life. Simply and clearly, he said,

"You can choose your thoughts."

His suggestion changed my life. It can change yours too.

The Power of Thought Can Save a Life

One of the worst situations a person can experience is being a prisoner of war.

I'm sure you have read or heard many horror stories of life as a prisoner of war in WWII. While millions of Jews died in the horrific conditions of the concentration camps, there were also some who survived. What was true for everyone at every moment in their terrible experience was each person had a choice—they could still choose their thoughts.

Viktor Frankl was a man who survived three Nazi death camps because he understood he had the freedom to choose his thoughts, regardless of the horrible conditions he was stuck in. In his bestselling book, Man's Search For Meaning, he wrote:

"Everything can be taken from a man, but...the last of the human freedoms—to choose one's attitude in any given set of circumstances, to choose one's own way."
-Viktor Frankl

No matter what the situation is, we have the free will and ability to intentionally choose our thoughts. You might notice others allow their negative thoughts to take over their lives. You can choose to intentionally change your thoughts. Frankly, it's much more enjoyable to be in control than let old thoughts control you.

Viktor Frankl chose to contemplate the image he carried of his beloved wife and to focus on his spirituality. He found the escape he needed from the desolation of his daily life by taking control of his thoughts. The Nazis could destroy many things, but were unable to control or destroy his thoughts. Viktor Frankl used his mind to help him adapt and ultimately become a survivor.

Not only can your thoughts help you to feel better in the moment, but your thoughts may also be the difference between death and life.

You Have Learned What You Didn't Learn in School

Throughout this book you have learned what stops you from moving forward in life are fears and limiting beliefs. Those fears are simply negative thoughts about something in the future which hasn't happened.

The opposite of each negative thought is the thought of your desired outcome. Both of these thoughts are thoughts about the future so you get to choose which you want. You've learned how to create powerful personal statements which allow you to focus on your desired outcome in a way that is believable. This believability is necessary for your subconscious mind to accept the outcome you have intentionally chosen.

You'll find it's much easier to achieve success when you believe in the outcome you desire, rather than when you are using your mental willpower to push against worries, anxiety and limiting beliefs to achieve your goals.

Most important is you've learned the benefits of being in control and intentionally changing your thoughts. When you are facing situations over which you have no control, you can easily use your powerful personal statements to reduce your stress. Reducing stress and feeling good in the moment are added benefits to powerful thinking.

Choosing to take control of your thoughts is something you can do anytime you want. No one can take this away from you. The more you control your thoughts, the better you'll feel.

My wish for you is you take what you have learned in Powerful Thinking on Purpose, use it daily, and share it with your friends, relatives, and your children. The concepts you have learned in this book are not taught in school and every person can benefit from them tremendously, regardless of age.

One important fact to remember: Powerful Thinking, positive thinking, and self-talk are not magic pills. Repetition is required for your success! When you use these tools on a regular basis, you'll notice how much better you feel. An added benefit is the more you use them, the less you'll worry, stress, or feel anxious.

Think of Powerful Thinking as the easy way to keep your mind fit - just like you keep your body fit.

To get you started I've created easy-to-use worksheets. You'll find them at the end of this book. These worksheets can help you motivate yourself.

This is a great time to think of what you may have been putting off or what you want to start. You can now accomplish your goal more easily because you know how to create and use your Powerful Personal Statement.

The good news is you have already begun to incorporate these new concepts at your subconscious level just by reading this book.

Just imagine the amazing directions your life can take when you use Powerful Thinking on Purpose...

NOW YOU KNOW

Make sure your thoughts always reflect your desires because your life will always go in the direction of your thoughts.

You can choose to create wonderful thoughts which make you feel good, or you can choose to allow negative thoughts to make you feel miserable. You are always in control. What you think and imagine is your choice.

Appendix

Powerful Thinking on Purpose™ Worksheets

Rules for Powerful Personal Statements:

1. Your statement must <u>be in the present tense.</u>
2. Your statement must <u>be positive.</u>
3. Your statement must <u>be simple.</u>
4. Your statement must <u>be believable.</u>
5. Your statement must <u>have a reward.</u>
6. Your statement must <u>feel true for you.</u>
7. If it's not true for you, include the 5 Powerful Words: <u>I like the idea that…</u>

SAMPLE POWERFUL PERSONAL STATEMENT IDEAS

Below are some helpful and powerful words you can use to create your personal statements. Of course, you can make up your own too. These are phrases just to get you started.

Remember to add the 5 Powerful Words in front of your personal statement if you need them. You can mix and match the ones from each column. Feel free to make up ones that suit your situation.

Use these at the beginning	**Use these words at the end**
I like the idea that	and I have more energy
I allow myself	and I feel great
I choose to	and I am calm and relaxed
It's easy for me	and I am proud of myself
Every time I	and I feel satisfied
I take time to	and I feel wonderful
Every day I	and I feel empowered

Personal Statement Examples:

Every day I look forward to training and I feel energized.

It's easy for me to focus and I am proud of myself.

Every time I golf I am calm and relaxed.

I like the idea that I easily stay safe and I feel great.

And you can use this any time:

I like the idea every day in every way I'm getting better and better!

Personal Goal Worksheets

Take a moment to think of some personal goals small or large, you want to achieve. These can be smaller goals, such as organizing your workspace, or larger goals, for example, improving your strength or speed, or getting a college degree.

Depending on what your goals are, some may have only one step, while others may have three or more tasks associated with them.

During the process of completing what you need to do, you might find some steps get delayed while you wait for information or responses from others. You may find you need to add more steps you hadn't thought of when you first began the process.

You might want to consider working on only one goal at a time until you get used to your new practice. Make your first ones fairly easy so you can show yourself how effortless and simple it is to use Powerful Thinking on Purpose to achieve your desires.

EXAMPLE

THREE GOALS I WANT TO ACHIEVE:

1. Find the best trainer for me
2. Get on the Team
3. Get over fears about speaking

Write Goal #1 below. Think of ways you can break it down into small action steps and write them below too:

GOAL # 1: Find the best trainer for me
Which action steps do you need to take to achieve your goal?

- Write a list of all trainers I know
- Ask friends who they recommend
- Write down questions to ask when I meet with a trainer
- Schedule interviews
- Stop worrying about choosing the wrong trainer again

For Goal #1 write your powerful personal statement below. Refer to the Sample Powerful Personal Statement Ideas page if needed. After you have written your statement, ask yourself the following questions:

Personal Statement: It's easy to find the perfect trainer and I feel great.

- ✓ Is it stated in the present?
- ✓ Is it positive?
- ✓ Is it simple?
- ✓ Is it believable?
- ✓ Does it feel true?
- ✓ Does it have a reward?

Write your personal statement here:

I easily find the perfect trainer and I feel great.

Read your personal statement out loud three times. Ask yourself honestly how you feel reading the statement. On a scale of 1 to 100 percent, how believable is it? Notice what thoughts come up for you. Remember to pay attention to your thoughts and feelings as they may point to some personal resistance.

If it's not believable, write it again below, adding the 5 Powerful Words.

"I like the idea that…"

I like the idea I easily find the perfect trainer and I feel great.

Read both statements and circle the one which feels most true for you.

GENERAL REMINDERS

✓ Repeat your powerful personal statement ten times in the morning and ten times in the evening.

✓ Continue every day while you are working on action steps A, B, C, and D. (If you find an action step difficult, create a Powerful Personal Statement to help you complete it.)

✓ Write down your powerful personal statement for additional reinforcement.

✓ Use the Widescreen TV Technique, or create your own technique. It's important to pretend to imagine how it will be when you reach your goal. Any way you do this is fine as long as you elicit a wonderful feeling. You get the same benefit whether you feel it or pretend to feel it.

✓ Remember: SEE, FEEL, and HEAR yourself. If you need to, start by pretending to imagine you have you have already achieved your goal. It works either way.

✓ After you have completed your goal, or your actions have become so natural you no longer need to reinforce them, give yourself a pat on the back, and move on to your next goal.

What do you want to do that you have put off? What would you like to accomplish this month? What would you like to achieve this year?

You now understand the steps to create your Powerful Personal Statement. You are ready to get started!

Grab a pen right now and write down three things you would like to do in the space below. It doesn't matter if your goals seem frivolous or are serious.

If you prefer, you can print out extra worksheets here:
www.thecenterofsuccess.com/powerfulthinking/

PERSONAL WORKSHEET

THREE GOALS I WANT TO ACHIEVE

1. _____

2 _____

3 _____

Write Goal #1 below. Think of ways you can break it down into small action steps and write them below too.

GOAL # 1:

_____

What action steps do you need to take to achieve your goal?

A) _____

B) _____

C) _____

D)_____

For <u>Goal #1</u> write your powerful personal statement below. Refer to the Sample Powerful Personal Statement Ideas page if needed. After you have written your statement, ask yourself the following questions:

Personal Statement:

_____

_____

✓Is it stated in the present?
✓Is it positive?
✓Is it simple?
✓Is it believable?
✓Does it feel true?
✓Does it have a reward?

Read your personal statement out loud three times. Ask yourself honestly how you feel reading the above statement. On a scale of 1 to 100 percent, how believable is it? Notice what thoughts come up for you. Notice any thoughts that may point to some personal resistance.

If it's not believable, write it again below, adding the 5 Powerful Words.

"I like the idea that…"

_____   _____

_____

Read both statements and write the one which feels most true for you here:

_____

REMINDER: Print out extra worksheets here:
 www.thecenterofsuccess.com/powerfulthinking/

After you have completed your goal or your actions have become so natural you no longer need to reinforce them, give yourself a pat on the back, and move on to your next goal. Remember, it's normal to have negative thoughts, it's what you do with them which makes all the difference.

Now, get out there and do great things!

RESOURCES

www.TheCenterOfSuccess.com:

Learn how private sessions can help you achieve your goals, eliminate fears, and improve your life. (The book you have just read includes only a tiny portion of the benefits of sessions with me.)

www.SportsRecoveryHypnosis.com

Improve your performance, or recover from the worries, stress, traumas, or injuries that hold you back. Learn how personal sessions with our team can turn your life around.

www.hypnotherapytrainer.com/learn-hypnosis
Interested in becoming a Certified Hypnotist with The National Guild of Hypnotists? Sign up here for 4 free videos and learn everything you need to know about Wendy Merron's Hypnotherapy Certification Course.

ACKNOWLEDGMENTS

A big thank you to the awesome friends who have supported me and continue to be my friends through thick and thin: Avis Yuni, Valerie Holiday, Becky Wagner, Holly Henry, Julia Ware, Justin Turpin, Grace Capuzzi, and David Fink. I am grateful to call each my friend.

A number of wonderful teachers have guided me on my path: Jeannie Bengston, who taught the Silva Mind Control class back in 1980 in Philadelphia; David Crump, who facilitated the Essential Experience Workshop in 2001; and my instructors and colleagues at The National Guild of Hypnotists.

Thank you to all my past, present, and future students who are excited to learn the craft of Hypnosis, Hypnotherapy, and Powerful Thinking. You are so appreciated.

A warm loving thank you to my children, Ariel, and Maddie Goldenthal. I have learned so much from you and I am grateful to be your mom.

My editor, is an accomplished and creative writer and daughter extraordinaire, Ariel Goldenthal, was extremely patient and did a fantastic job at editing and formatting my book. She always understands exactly what I wanted to convey, and she edited with gentleness, humor, and insight.

Last, I want to *thank you* for reading my book. I encourage you to use what you have learned to take control of your thoughts, feelings, and actions.

You've got this.

Made in the USA
Middletown, DE
28 September 2023

39550790R00115